SUNFLOWERS

Jassmine James

PublishNation, London
www.publishnation.co.uk

Dedicated to Shirley "Whirley" Williams. I bet your talking the ears off the angels. I'll see you later. (Thanks Shirl).

All the hardworking Mediums, Healers and people who are of service with love.

Thanks to Lucinda Stockton for editing, making sense of all my gibberish.

Last but not least Jennifer Harter of Harter Art Creations harter.art.creations@gmail.com

Sunflowers is also dedicated to Charlotte Hecquet. You are one of the brightest stars in the sky. Lots of love Char Char xxx

Chapters

Foreword

I have the pleasure and good fortune to have known Jassmine James for a number of years now, both as a friend and on a professional level.

Jassmine is a most gifted accurate psychic, who provides excellent life guidance with her intelligent insight and mediumship.

She is very sincere and has helped many of my friends and family; all have been astounded by her knowledge of current situations in their lives. As we all are aware, and have experienced, there are many twists and turns in life, some good and some challenging. Jassmine certainly has the ability to tap into what may help one find inner peace and strength.

Good luck Jassmine with your wonderful book, which will indeed reach out and help many more people.

Lots of love

Sheila Ryan

CHAPTER 1

CHURCH TAKE ME HOME
THE MOTHER RETURNS

November 2007. The Dream.

I am standing in front of a church built from thick white stone. The doors have ornate patterns lovingly carved into the wood. I touch the huge gold handles and push one of the doors open. I step inside, closing the door behind me. The church has a low ceiling, which is arched and has the look of a cave more than a place of worship. The altar has tea lights and candles burning brightly, lighting the way for God to come and sit in His home. His son, Jesus, is nailed to the cross which hangs from the ceiling, his head bowed. There is a stab wound in his side and a crown of thorns majestically envelope his head; a bloody tear on his cheek, his eyes closed in repose.

The pews are empty.

I stand rooted to the spot, not knowing why I am there, or what I am supposed to do in this dream. The walls are painted a light green and I think to myself "What a strange colour to paint a church". I close my eyes and feel a sensation blowing through me – a wind that threatened to touch my soul, steal it away and hold me imprisoned for ever in this place. My arms have goosebumps.

I open my eyes and notice a person sitting in the front pew on the left hand side. She is wearing a large black hat and her head is turned slightly, as if aware she is being watched. A veil is draped across her face but her eyes are visible. I want to turn and run but I am trapped in this dream – however hard I try to wake myself up. A sense of unease descends.

She turns her shoulders to look at me properly, her eyes unblinking. They hold no life, no promise of tomorrow. She stands up and slowly floats up the aisle towards me; then her feet land on the stone clad floor with a thud. The black high heeled shoes echo around the walls of the church. She is wearing a knee-length black lacy dress, her long lean legs poking out from under the skirt as she comes closer. I glance at her chest and see the altar candles through her body. She is a ghost. Her arms are hanging unnaturally, black lace gloves clad her long fingers and I can see her red nail varnish through the delicate pattern of the lace. I cannot move. The fear rises in my stomach, bile fills my mouth. All the old feelings that I had experienced from my childhood are flooding back to me. She comes even closer and I close my eyes, praying to God to save me. Her eyes are deadpan, still unblinking, staring directly into mine. Without averting her gaze she steps to my right, leans forward and breathes into my face, an ethereal white vapour billowing from her mouth. I cough, trying not to inhale it. She steps away from me and suddenly floats into the air, spinning round and round, before dropping back to the floor, opening the church door and slamming it shut.

* * * * * * * * * *

As I opened my eyes from the dream, slowly adjusting to the darkness of the room, I fumbled for the light. I switched it on, knowing that my Mother had died because she had just come to tell me so.

CHAPTER 2

ORANGES

Life as a working medium is never easy. My phone would ring from the wee small hours of the morning until late at night. For example, a client once phoned me at 2.00 a.m. She was bright and breezy as she enthusiastically tried to book her appointment. She didn't get any sense out of me; I sounded like someone from the living dead. I grunted at her, made sure she was okay, told her to call me later in the morning - and put the phone down.

Some clients came out of curiosity and others came because they had lost someone dear to them, either through illness or even murder. At all times I had to be on my A Game, having trust in Bob (my Native American Guide) and the Angels that surround us. For those of you who have read 'Rainbows' you will already know Bob very well; however, I will give you all a refresher in Chapter 3.

The readings at times can be so funny. There is laughter through tears, and even a few "I'm sorrys" from the spirits that come through. This helps everybody on both sides. For the client it is liberating to hear the apology they never received in their lifetime, and for the sprit it frees them to go on and progress in the spiritual realms. There is no death, just a shift of dimensions.

In 1994 I had just begun my journey into being a medium and, looking back, I cannot believe that anybody came to see me as my readings were so very long.

Drama was my middle name. In my mind I was Whoopie Goldberg's character, Oda Mae, from the film 'Ghost'. Eyes closed, duly moving my head, opening one eye to see if the client was still there. I am sure that they nearly died of boredom waiting for a message. Lack of confidence in my abilities, and always second guessing myself took its toll. Bob would come through and say "Trust Child, we believe in who you are and who we are to you. You can never go wrong within yourself".

It was all right for Bob to say, he was floating about, without a body. No life experiences to be bothered about – he had done all that. At that time I felt embarrassed of who I was (and getting paid for it, when I was getting it free). Self-confidence had been lacking since my childhood, so I was working through that. But my abilities had been there since I remembered being in my incubator and catching glimpses of my Father through the glass. Yes folks, if you've just picked up *Sunflowers* for the first time and haven't heard of me before, please read *Rainbows* first as it will explain to you the early years of my life and how I became who I am today.

However, miraculously, the people who had come to see me would tell their friends and others, and I became busier and busier. My son, Joshua, was coming up to three years of age. Travis, his dad, was still flitting in and out of our lives, never really committing to either of us. He was a businessman, whose first love was his work and any female who had a pulse. He was akin to the man who says "Baby, I fuck *her*, but I make love to *you!*" Rose coloured glasses can be fantastic. I was the one he "made love" to and he saw his son when he visited. What more could a girl want?

Only time would make me see the truth and when I took off those rose tinted glasses, and grew a pair of fat hairy balls, I saw the light of day. I held my own counsel and changed the way I wanted to be treated by a man. Travis was not it. But, for the time being, I loved him unconditionally. I would have leapt over mountains for him, chased the wolves from his door – you get the picture?

CHAPTER 3

BOB

Bob is my Native American Guide. Obviously Bob was not his Earth name but it's what I call him. He has been my constant teacher throughout my life. I know it's hard for sceptics to understand but Bob is as real to me as any living human. The only difference being is that he doesn't have the Earthly responsibilities that we do. He is free to teach me about the greatness of the spiritual life that is here on Earth.

You must be crazy to think that this is it, this is all we have. Our material life. Our substance. I know there is so much more, thanks to Bob. I have seen it and it's beautiful. The dreams, the visions, the proof that has been shown to me is all down to my Guide.

Bob's physical appearance is quite something. He is tall, with flowing long black hair, high cheek bones and deep set brown eyes. He belonged to the Sioux tribe, Band, in the Black Hills of Dakota. He was from a long line of well respected Medicine Shamans and continued what his forefathers had begun. He was a great warrior; but he also loved to dance. He is gentle and protective with me, but can be as fierce as a bear if a spirit steps out of line. Without him I don't know where I would be.

From what I can gather, I am Bob's assignment. Apparently it had all been sorted a long time before I was born, that he would teach the World as much as he could through me; I agreed to work with him. He doesn't manifest himself through my body; not like Silver Birch did to Maurice Barbenell.

Briefly, Maurice [then an eighteen year old journalist] was sent to write an article on a Spiritualist Circle. As an atheist, Maurice found it hilarious to see a Chinese Guide manifest himself.

The following week, he went back and continued his article. [Incidentally he had been told by a Guide the previous week that he would be doing this before long]. When he found himself stirring from a deep sleep he apologised for his rudeness, but everyone was staring at him. He had fallen into a trance and Silver Birch had manifested himself in Barbenell's body. He said that he had been training for this for years and that Barbenell would be working with the Spirit World in the future. And that was indeed the case until Barbenell's passing.

Whilst some of you may be saying "Oh yeah?", whilst Maurice was in his trance, Silver Birch told the Circle to stick a pin deep into his arm. When Maurice came out of his trance there was no sign of injury.

Silver Birch not only gave much information about the Spirit World, he taught thousands on how to love without judgement and to take every Earthly experience as an advantage to their souls to gain Spiritual strength.

This is what Bob teaches also. He has shown me that however fucked off I get with a situation, or what I think is a disaster, it is actually an opportunity for my soul to progress. I have snapped at him that he doesn't have a body so get off my case! But he will smile and send me love until I calm down, and then he will teach.

For his part, it takes a lot of effort for a Guide to talk to us stupid humans. It takes unconditional love and an emission of light-filled energy to guide the path of our soul. The thought, the intuition, the dreams are helped by your inner voice and your Guides that are around you.

Bob is brilliant in his teachings. He comes close to me whenever I've got a quiet moment, for example walking Chef (my dog) through nature. He will fall into step with me and teach me something profound. In my readings Bob is never far away. As I'm talking I can see him lining up the spirits to talk to me. He looks as if he is on fast-forward. His vibration is a much higher frequency than mine or the Earth's. In fact, because of matter, we are quite slow whereas Bob is free from that.

Bob will help me with my train of thought regarding spiritual awareness – even in the writing of this book, which requires a deep understanding. He has also helped me to teach others. I haven't mentioned my Earthly qualifications or achievements, although I could, but this is about the soul.

Bob has a great sense of humour. For example, when Joshua was a toddler I took him a posh restaurant with starched white tablecloths and heavy crystal glasses. It definitely was not child-friendly but, as it was a special occasion, nothing could be said. Or so I thought.

Joshua was eating Spaghetti Bolognese and, like any child, he was getting some of it on to the tablecloth. He then accidentally knocked over a glass of water which went into his dinner and splashed all over the table. It looked like a murder scene! I got up to apologise to the waitress but she had already seen it and shouted "Can't you control your child?"

The restaurant fell silent, and a red mist descended. All I could see was her mouth moving in slow motion. I was just about to snap back at her when I saw Bob standing next to me, saying "Now you can lose your temper, but then this person has won the argument. She already thinks that you and your child are savages so, if you play into her hands, all will be lost". He put a Totem Pole behind her and I saw the waitress climb it and then slide down. He continued "If you shout back she will climb the pole and look down on you in her righteousness. However, if you stay silent, see what happens". Again the woman tried to climb the pole but it was greasy. "The grease is your indifference. Let it go, and see her judgement and ignorance be revealed to all".

I stood my ground in silence while she continued to shout about Josh. Then she stopped mid-sentence and I could see by her expression that she felt stupid. She had belittled herself without me having to say a word.

I said quietly "I would like you to clean the table and my son requires another meal. Thank you".

She did as she was asked and apologised for the way she had spoken to me. I nodded but said nothing.

Did she get a tip? Not really but, thanks to Bob stepping in, I kept my dignity.

CHAPTER 4

LOOK FOR THE STARS AND YOU MIGHT JUST GET THE MOON

I was living in an apartment and, even though it was spacious, it had no access to a garden. I wanted Joshua to have some space to run around. At that time, my friend Julia was living around the corner and when I visited her, I would take a shortcut down Bungalow Road in South Norwood, London. There was a house up for rent which had stood unoccupied for over a year. I knew the house was waiting for me. I talked to Travis and my friends about it but my mind was already made up. I wanted to move there.

The house had three bedrooms and a little garden front and back. It was just right. I made a few enquiries and within the next few days I found myself viewing the house. I liked it instantly. Although there were outlines of many spirit people moving in and out of the shadows, the house had a nice vibration. The owners had been very happy there but had moved to warmer climes. They were relieved to have the place rented and practically threw the keys at me.

Within six weeks we had moved into Bungalow Road and Josh loved having a garden. I kept my telephone number so clients could still book in for readings, and so started a new chapter in my life.

CHAPTER 5

CIRCLES, GO ROUND IN

A Spiritual Circle is when a medium runs a development group. An Open Circle is one where anyone can attend each week. A Closed Circle is by invitation only. A Closed Circle tends to build up the spiritual energy more intensely because the sprits get to know the people who come each and every week, and can communicate more easily. It is like us getting to know a friend over the years. You know their smile and can recognise their laughter out of a group of people.

Bob had told me I was going to be joining a circle soon, a closed one. Even though I had sat in on an open circle, I had never been to a closed one before. I spoke to Bob and said "Where is the closed circle, Bob? I thought you were sorting it out".

"Patience Child, trust in me".

"It's all right for you Bobby – no bills, no day to day living. You don't even have to pee!"

"But Child, I have to learn, to help and teach you, I might not have the day to day rigours of your Earthly functions, but I am here to teach you. And helping you helps me progress. And teaching you has its own un-Earthly challenges!"

Bob faded away from my mind and left me to ponder about him finding it a challenge to guide me. He certainly had drawn the spiritual short straw. But all I knew for certain was that, through it all, Bob loved me, loved my soul's energy and I loved him just as much. Anyway, enough of the love-in.

Julia phoned me and asked if wanted to have a reading with an accomplished medium called Stacey. She was a professional reader with a good reputation through word of mouth. Julia went to her for a reading and afterwards told me that Stacey was true to her reputation. After she read me, Stacey suggested that I should be in a circle. I told her I didn't know who ran one and she smiled and said "I do. I run a closed circle on Mondays between 7 and 9pm at my home. Would you like to join?"

"Yes of course".

"That's great, I'll see you then."

"Should I bring anything?"

"Just yourself," she laughed.

I could see Bob hovering over Stacey's head as she turned to open the door to let me out. I poked my tongue out at Bob and winked him a smile.

I couldn't wait for Monday to come. The people who attended it came from all walks of life - teachers, nurses and a dustbin man. The soul, it seems, is not aware of class or colour – thank goodness.

After the introductions we all sat round the table. Stacey sat at the head. To open the Circle, she made us hold hands while she said a prayer. Then, still holding hands we meditated for a while to build up the energy. I began to feel restless. I sensed hands touching my shoulders and face. I opened my eyes and saw orbs of light dancing around my head and a feeling of exhilaration filled me.

Stacey was training some of the students to stand on platform, which means standing in front of an audience or congregation, either in a Spiritualist church or a church hall. When they stood up in the Circle it helped the students build up their confidence in preparation for their work.

A nervous woman stood up, closed her eyes and started to read one of the people in the Circle. She was precise and confident in connecting the person to her "dead" relatives. I was impressed. I was trying to get something from the spirit world but I was completely blocked. It was like my airways were not in tune. So I just let it go, and watched and learned about others and how they connected to spirits. Even though there was a common thread amongst us, we contact the other side in different ways. Each and every one of us has a unique personality – one size does not fit all.

Stacey asked whether I could sense anything; I still couldn't. Then she suggested that I closed my eyes, which I did. I felt a slight shift in the back of my head. A little light pulsated and then exploded, after which I found myself in a cornfield. The corn was waving in the wind, its ears pointing to the sun. Children started to appear amongst the corn, jumping high and floating in the air. I smiled up at them and one of them hovered above my head, her golden curls framing her face her heartshaped face, her brown eyes twinkling. She reached down and pulled me into the air. I flew with the children, high in the sky. We touched the Sun and went behind it.

Then the children gently guided me down to the river and sunk my feet into the water.

The children stopped giggling and became serious. They floated away and disappeared. I looked at the water and it began to ripple. A man's head emerged, his forehead visible above the water, his eyes were closed. Then he slowly opened them and rested his on mine. I started to cry and was vaguely aware of someone wiping away my tears. He walked out of the water towards me. He looked dry, his long dark hair fell around his shoulders and his white robes hung loosely around his body.

He stood in front of me and gently pressed his finger into the middle of my head. As he did this he said "Learn Child. Learn all about us for there are many worlds within your world. Times and places of the soul are timeless, endless. We will come to you and teach you all we can".

Then the vision disappeared and I found myself back in the Circle. The students were looking at me. Stacey asked "Do you realise you were talking us through what you were saying?"

"No. I had no idea".

"That vision of yours was to help you understand more about the Spirit World; and to learn more about the Circle".

And as I attended the Circle more my skills as a medium developed. As I read more it helped me learn what the messages were saying to me. Between the Circle and Bob, I was improving slowly. I relaxed about all things spiritual, and stopped being cynical. However, Bob was just about to make me give up something I didn't want to.

CHAPTER 6

SMOKIN' ACES

Smoking. I loved it. It's stupid really, because when I began to smoke I would get so dizzy and nauseous I would fall over or throw up. But I persevered and now it was a habit.

Bob constantly told me "How can we give you messages when we have to deal with your body's energies?"

"What are you talking about? The messages get understood by the people I read for. "

He chuckled. Once again my stubborn behaviour never bothered Bob. He always found it amusing. He was far ahead of the game. "Whenever you smoke, Child, a blanket of energy surrounds your body, like a brick wall and it is hard for the message to be received from me to you. Look, I'll show you. "

I closed my eyes and as I sat back in my chair I could see myself sitting on a patch of grass. Bob stood behind me, arms folded, and delivered his message from his mind to mine. I watched the energy travel up my spine, over the back of my head and into the middle of my forehead. He then began to send another message but just as it was about to travel up my spine a brown thick liquid was tipped over my body and the message fell to the ground, its energy broken.

Bob said "Now do you understand Child? You only get part of the message because the body's energies can't get through. You will see so much better if you didn't smoke."

To justify my habit, I said "I know plenty of people who smoke and are really good mediums".

"But they are not you. Your body's vibration does not take to it and you are going to give it up in the New Year".

It was Christmas and not long until New Year's Eve. I said "No I'm not Bob. You can't change who I am, what I'm about. I'd like to see you try!"

Bob stepped away and wouldn't be drawn into the subject as to how he would stop me from 'smokin''. Like most people that have habits they don't think that they have one. But I did. Joshua was still small and even though I smoked outside or when he was asleep, it still wasn't good enough. I smelt like an ashtray – my hair, my clothes, the rooms in the house. New Year's Eve was near. Travis and I celebrated with a bottle of wine and a cigarette.

We then went to bed. When I woke up the next morning I reached for the cigarettes, put one in my mouth and nearly hurled all over the back garden wall. I felt dizzy and weak. I tried again. The same thing happened. I felt so ill; my skin was clammy and my heart was pumping like a piston.

I threw the cigarette on the floor and walked back into the kitchen. I leant against the cupboard and folded my arms. "Okay Bob, you win, but I will be trying again". I could feel his energy around me.

He said "Please do. Help yourself Child", but I couldn't. I tried and tried but I couldn't smoke so I gave up, and haven't smoked for fifteen years.

CHAPTER 7

EVOLUTION OF THE STAR CHILD

Joshua was now coming up to 4 years old, and displaying signs of spiritual awareness. Only time would tell whether or not he kept his ability as he got older. So often children who tell their families they have seen "Auntie So and So" or "Grandma from Wiltshire" are ridiculed, or told it was a dream, even if they recognise old photos.

Joshua would not have that problem. If he saw, I would listen to what he had to say. And this happened when a friend of mine, Georgie, came over for a chat. She had lost her Uncle Derek a few years before and was still upset about his passing. Whenever Georgie came over, Uncle Derek would make his presence felt with me by standing behind her. He was a tall slim man who still liked to wear his black round glasses. His small round eyes would sparkle with the same vibrant energy he once had on Earth. He had been very close to his niece when he was alive, and in death nothing had changed. Georgie and I were chatting away and I could feel Uncle Derek floating around listening to our conversation. I didn't say anything to Georgie. Instead I went to the kitchen to make a cup of tea and then went upstairs to the loo.

When I came back down, Georgie was as white as a sheet. I joked "The tea isn't that bad is it?"

Georgie blinked, turned her head and motioned for me to come to the kitchen. Her face was paralysed with fear, her elfin features looked sharp and her big blue eyes were on stalks. Joshua was playing quietly with his toys on the floor. In the kitchen, Georgie said "Joshua told me that Uncle Derek was sitting next to me on the sofa. I then asked what he looked like and he said 'he is wearing glasses'. It's all right coming from you – I'm used to it. But from your son! My goodness, it frightened the crap out of me!"

I smiled. "If he says any more about Derek, smile sweetly and just accept what he's said. Don't make a big fuss about it. I don't want him to think that he's some sort of alien from Mars. He's a child that is in tune with the Universe". I called out to Josh "You all right Josh? Do you want a drink?" He shook his head. I closed the door and said "Georgie, go back into the sitting room and just act as if nothing's happened".

CHAPTER 8

THE C WORD AND MY MOTHER

My new clients were coming to me through word of mouth. They lived all over the country and I was amazed how far the word was spreading. The stipulation was that the client came on recommendation from a person I had already read. The phone rang and a woman was asking me whether she could book in for a reading. I asked her the usual and she told me her name was Yvette. I booked her in for the following afternoon.

When she arrived, I opened the door to her and her eyes widened. She said "You look just like your Mother, Cynthia. You look as if you've been spat out of her mouth". My heart sank as I motioned for her to sit down at the table in the lounge. "I live near your Mother in Peckham. I know you don't see her, but I see that your sister Diane lives there".

My heart was racing. My fucking Mother - still haunting me by default. She would never leave me alone. "It's all right love, I don't want to talk about your Mum. I'm here to see if you can get in contact with someone. I have their ring and nobody has worn it since I took it off them when they took their last breath". She lovingly unwrapped the tissue paper enclosing the ring, and handed it to me.

"No pressure". I thought. But all the time I was thinking about my Mother. I held the ring and tried to tune in but I just could not do it. Then I saw the hope behind Yvette's eyes and could not deny her. I put my feelings aside and closed my eyes. I could see a young woman lying in a hospital bed; she opened her eyes and smiled at me and told me her name, then stepped out of her bed and stood next to it. She looked well now. She looked as if she were only in her 30s when she passed. I relayed everything that I saw to Yvette. She nodded. I described her and Yvette said that it was her daughter. I looked at her and said "What would you like to say to your Mother?"

"Cunt. Say 'cunt' to my Mother".

"Excuse me, what did you say?"

"Say cunt to her. She'll definitely know that it's me. "

I refused, and so she refused to show me anything else. I asked Bob; he was silent. I told him "Thanks".

I looked at the curious Mother with a pained expression on my face. Yvette said "Go on love, tell me some more, tell me that she's all right".

"I'm sorry I can't read any more".

"No love, you're not telling me the truth. I know you've got more".

Her daughter was laughing hard. "You've got to tell my Mum what I said".

I replied "Don't say it any more. Besides if I tell her that word she's going to punch my lights out".

"No she won't. She will definitely know it's me. For fuck's sake, tell her what I bloody said!"

I took a deep breath and said "Cunt. She's saying 'cunt' to you". I put my hands to my face and I'm not ashamed to say I shed a tear. Yvette stared at me. I was ready for the punch but it didn't come because she roared with laughter.

"That's my girl! That's her! I should have had a wreath made in that word. She said it all the time. But you know what? You could eat off her kitchen floor – she was the cleanest girl ever. She dressed smartly and her son wore the latest gear. But she had a mouth on her".

And through Yvette's tears the reading went on without any more hitches. But the burning question for me was – would I ever get any peace from my Mother?

CHAPTER 9

SPRING SONG

Joshua was growing up before my eyes. He was at school in Year 1 and loved it. We walked a good mile before school and that gave us a chance to talk along the way. We picked up some of Joshua's friends en route.

Winter was drawing in and Joshua was getting tired of walking to school, so I got a car. Josh's intuition was getting stronger and it showed. One morning, as I was just about to put the key in the ignition, he said "It's not going to work".

"No it's fine, it worked yesterday". I turned the key but, sure enough, that hunk of metal was not going anywhere.

Joshua looked lazily out of the window and said "It's still not going to work Mum".

I got out of the car and thought "He's got it; I just hope he will be able to cope with his psychic abilities and not suffer".

We went back indoors and I called the school to tell them we would be late as the car had broken down.

CHAPTER 10

THE CRIMINAL ELEMENT

Lin is a friend of mine and a great medium. She reads for people who need a lot of help. Drug dealers, drug addicts, the 'Criminal Element'.

Lin had a spiritual shop in Thornton Heath High Street in South London. She had rooms above which mediums and healers could hire for consultations. Lin sold candles, crystals and tarot cards, and everything else in-between.

This particular day, Joshua and I were walking in the shop and Carly, one of Lin's four children, was standing behind the counter. I said "Hello" and asked her where Lin was.

"Upstairs", she replied. I asked her to look after Josh while I went upstairs to speak to Lin.

I bellowed up the stairs "Lin, it's me, Jaz, can I come up?"

"Yeah Jaz, come up".

I could hear other people's voices, but a man's voice stood out from the rest. I could hear him say "Yeah you fucking cunt!" Everyone around him laughed. I walked into the room full of men, and Lin was sitting behind her desk to the left.

I said "Hello" and gave her a hug. Then I whispered "Who are they?"

I recognised one of them – let's call him 'Danny'. He was Lin's other daughter's boyfriend. Lin had figured to keep an eye on her daughter she had to embrace Danny and his friends. It wasn't ideal but it had to be done. That, or lose her daughter. For all his naughty ways, I liked Danny although not for the life that he had chosen. He had jet black hair and green eyes, and was as bright as a button with a wicked sense of humour.

He was number two to his boss. Danny took care of business, sorted out the crap on the street and reported back to his boss, who happened to be sitting in the room. Danny said "Hello Jaz, all right?"

"Yeah Danny. You?" It's like the *'Long Good Friday'* in here!"

Danny roared with laughter. His boss - let's call him 'Kenny' - was sitting in the corner of the room. He owned his space and he was staring straight at me. His eyes followed everything I did. Then he spoke.

"Are you the girl that does them readings? Do me one".

"No thanks mate, I've just come up to see Lin," I replied.

I turned to look at Lin. We both laughed at the same time. It's nice when someone knows you that well. That laugh meant so many things, one being 'I would rather jump off the nearest building than do a reading for you!' I pulled up a chair and Lin and I fell into our friendship shorthand, as only open hearts and kinship can experience.

Kenny persisted. "I want a reading from you".

24

"I'm not reading today".

He said again "But I want a reading".

I ignored him and looked at Lin and raised an eyebrow. She threw her head back and chuckled, lit a cigarette and glanced over at Kenny. "You can either read him and teach him a lesson, or just leave now and that's that".

I got up to go.

Kenny asked once more.

I told him "I can't. I'm not in that frame of mind".

Kenny smirked. "I bet you can't do it".

"You're absolutely right. I can't do it today", I told him.

"What will it take? How much money do you charge?"

"I said … I'm not reading today".

Lin interjected "You know what Jaz. Teach him a lesson, he thinks it's all a big joke. Just read him".

I sighed. "Give me your keys. I need them to connect with you". Sometimes when I read a client I would hold their keys or a watch to connect with them more. This practice is called psychometry (I have since stopped doing it; I now only read Tarot cards).

Instead, he tried to hand me his gun. It was shiny silver and white – and deadly in the wrong hands. I shook my head and walked towards the door in disgust.

He sighed. "I'm sorry love. I didn't mean to offend you. I'm just showing off in front of my boys".

I was now angry enough to do a reading and he relented, handing me his keys. I held them and closed my eyes. I could hear his cronies laughing and he told them to "Shut the fuck up".

I tuned in. Above his head to the left there was an energy – a woman was forming. She spoke "Say to him Mary's here".

"That's my Grandmother! She was called Mary".

Mary went on to tell me of a terraced house with a big garden that had nothing but junk – scraps of metal. It was more like a salvage yard than a garden.

He whispered "All of us used to live there with my Nan". His eyes filled with tears. "That's exactly how the garden was. We used to keep our cars in the back as well".

"You gained a million and lost a million through owning a vineyard in Spain".

"Yes". He turned to his pals and asked "Have you been talking to her because if you have, it's not fucking funny".

Danny spoke up. "No Kenny. She's the real deal. Just shut up and let her talk".

Kenny growled "You can only talk to me like that once in your lifetime Danny, before I slap you silly. Sorry Princess – carry on".

I closed my eyes and said "Italy. There was a man who was killed there. His name begins with M". I clutched my throat. "He didn't die very well".

The colour from Kenny's face drained. He stood up and threw a wedge of money at me. He took the stairs two at a time and fell down the rest. He called up to his men to "Fuckin' hurry up and get in the fuckin' car!"

Danny looked at me and said "I would love to know what freaked him out. I've never seen him like that before. "

Kenny didn't speak to anyone for a week, and he refused to be drawn into any conversations about that day, but he did take his boys round to the house that had once belonged to his Nan. He sat outside the house for ages, his eyes rimmed with tears.

I can't tell you any more; I'll take that to my grave. But Kenny and Danny are now each doing a ten year stretch, as we speak.

CHAPTER 11

WILD HORSES

Mothers. Fathers. Who needs them? I was coming to that conclusion. Josh was nearly six years old and neither of my parents had anything to do with either of us. My Father would come into my dreams and then we would play catch-up on what he was up to. My Mother was too dangerous to be near, because she destroyed my life, even if she was a whisper away in my thoughts. I needed some family foundations, some rocks. My brother Louis was dealing with his own issues and I hadn't seen him for quite a while. I hadn't seen my sister Diane in years. Sometimes you have to break in life in order to heal and mend again. And that is exactly what happened to me.

Something in my soul had told me told me to go to Joshua's school early, and as I stood outside looking into the classroom I saw my son being dragged from the floor and on to his feet by a teacher's assistant. I stepped forward and pressed my face against the window of the classroom. The teacher's assistant saw me and dropped my son's arm from her firm grip. I wanted to beat her senseless! But if I had, I would be no better than her. Instead, I waited until everyone had collected their children, and asked a friend to look after Josh whilst I dealt with her. She felt so guilty that she had been caught out, she was attacking me, trying to defend and justify her actions. She practically had her finger up my nose.

Quietly I told her if she put her finger near my face again I might be tempted to bite it off. She stepped back from me. I contacted the 'powers-that-be' and not a thing was done about it. She had been an assistant for over 20 years and was a "pillar of the community". It was her word against mine, and the teacher told me she had "never seen Mrs T do anything like that", and "… it was not in her nature".

So I was called a 'liar'. I took Joshua out of the school and sent him to a private one. He would not have been taught properly at the previous school anyway because his parent had dared to kick up a fuss. I don't know whether this incident was the catalyst, or the last straw on the camel's back, but my past caught up with me in the most traumatic way.

Maybe I felt safe enough to let out my past, and the horrible fact that my Mother had tried to kill me when I was a child. But she was back spiritually and I was under attack. I was watching the television one day when the images suddenly faded away and the face of my Mother appeared on the screen. There was me as a child, lying face down spread-eagled on a bed whilst my Mother stood behind me, inserted a tube into my rectum and started to pour water into it. She did this to me, Louis and Diane on a regular basis. This image on the television screen came to life. I was seeing this horrific scene in 3D. I saw the horror and fear in my child-face. I could see the pink bedspread and my mouth biting it, wincing in pain. Tears were streaming down my face. I looked frightened and bewildered. Mum stopped what she was doing to me and caught my eye, then smiled.

I cried and tried to grapple with the remote control to turn the television off, but as I was doing this the television went back to its original channel and everything was back to normal. I crumpled into a heap on the sofa and sobbed my heart out. I didn't know what was going on. I felt completely isolated – raped by my own Mother. I could never get away from her – she haunted me and she wasn't even dead. People are far more frightening than spirits.

I didn't want to talk to anyone about what had happened. I am sure I could have but I didn't know how to articulate it. Flashbacks of my Mother's abuse were becoming more and more frequent. They would not only come when I was watching television, it could happen anywhere, any time. This continued for a few weeks until I finally broke and told a good friend about it. She didn't know what to say – all she could do was sit and listen. This was spiritual warfare – doctor's pills would not do anything for me, although I was sorely tempted.

I crawled into bed and fell asleep out of sheer exhaustion. Bob came into view, his handsome face smiling with only love emanating from his eyes. A feather was in his headdress, and he was standing in front of the beloved vast Earth plains that were looked after by his proud nation – the Sioux Tribe. He then leapt on to a horse, drew his fingers across his face which left painted lines and said "Whenever I had to go into battle I would put on my war paint and prepare my mind for the warfare. And if I was going to make my transition to the Happy Hunting Ground I would know that all was well on the Earth if I were to die".

"What does that mean Bob, what's your point?"

He smiled. "When you go into battle you have to face your enemies head on".

"What are you suggesting then?"

He touched my face and said "See your Mother".

CHAPTER 12

RAIN IN MY FACE

Just one minute's peace, that was all I wanted. But it wasn't to be. My only saving grace was Joshua. Through all the upset, he was as good as gold. He didn't give me a hard time, he just waited. And wait he would have to do.

Josh was doing well in his new private school in Purley, Surrey which made life easier. However, mentally I was on the floor, trying to fight, trying to deal with the flashbacks of the abuse my Mother had inflicted on me. During the day I looked after Joshua and worked. Work was anything from readings, cleaning or whatever else I could do. The word 'no' was not in my vocabulary – I just kept on going. After I finished my readings it was time for me to do battle with my flashbacks. Watching television was out of the question after the vision of horror that had appeared on the screen. So I read books, which I loved. But I couldn't concentrate. My whole body felt as if I had been run over by a truck. I had flu-like symptoms.

Maybe when I smoked in the past, I had managed to suppress all of these feelings – tucking them away with each puff. But now I had given up, those feelings were free to wander around unchecked. I would not smoke again – Bob had made sure of that! It was a spiritual shift that was going on. Maybe I needed to do this. But I couldn't get over it; I felt I was ready to die. My sensible head knew that was out of the question. What about Joshua?

However, the other side of me wanted peace. And the only way to get it was to stop breathing. I hated who I was, hated every part of me. Both parents could not stand me. Mum had thrown me out of the womb and Dad's indifference was a clever disguise to cover his emotions about how he really felt. To cover my own [emotions] I chose a weapon and, from the box of abuse, I declared a war on food. I ate to numb my feelings. I was eating up a storm and didn't care.

Abuse is a strange conundrum; the survivors always blame themselves. Thinking it is their fault for what parents, or whoever the perpetrator was, had done to them; maybe even feeling loved through it.

But on this night I was ready – ready to die. Now I know more than anyone that once you take your own life, and you wake on the other side, you are still the same person only you don't have the body that you destroyed. And you still have to go through many layers of healing to find your Heaven within. I had spoken to many who have done it and Bob had shown me what people go through when you have chosen to allow that to happen. It is a process of peeling away the layers and reaching the conclusion of self-love and then trying to help others on Earth stop doing that they did. However, at this particular moment, death seemed to be the answer.

I tucked Joshua into bed and read him a story. I decided I would not leave a note. I crept into the kitchen and pulled a sharp knife from the draw. I laid my wrist on the side of the counter and braced myself for the first cut. Then I heard Mavis' voice – the lady who had fostered me for 16 years and had sadly passed years ago when I was 18. And there she was, standing behind me.

She said "Where there's a will, there's a way. I brought you up to tough it out. Besides, the life you brought into this world didn't ask for his Mother to be taken so soon. Your son needs you, don't you dare leave him motherless. There are better times ahead for you, you *will* get through this".

I dropped the knife back in the drawer and closed it, before bursting into floods of tears. "What was I thinking?" I lay down on the kitchen floor and realised that the only way to get through this was to pick myself up, dig deep and start again. I crawled to the phone and dialled the Samaritans. I talked to them practically every night for two months. Thank God for them. Between Bob, Mavis and the kind words at the other end of phone, I stopped myself from ending it all.

CHAPTER 13

DOLPHIN - LEGACY

Bob still insisted that I see my Mother, but I just couldn't do it. I wasn't strong enough but, deep down, I knew that he was right. When, or how, I could face her only God knew.

I hadn't seen my brother Louis for months so when he contacted me it was fantastic, but as soon as I met up with him I knew something was wrong. We hugged each other and he said "All right sis?"

I nodded and asked "What's wrong?"

He started to cry. "It's Mum. She's in hospital – she's had a stroke. I can't do this on my own sis. She's in Guy's Hospital. I just need a bit of support. I thought you might want to see her before anything else happens".

I folded my arms across my chest, nodded and looked down at my feet. Maybe this was the time that Bob was talking about, although I instinctively knew it wasn't. I'm no angel but I couldn't confront someone who was so ill – that didn't sit right with me. Like I have said before I had never been rude to my Mother, I had treated her with the utmost respect; never lowering myself to her level. This was for my brother. Louis smiled. He had Mum's eyes and dimples. I pressed my finger into one of them and said "Okay, I'll go and see her".

CHAPTER 14

16 MOONS AGO

I had arranged to meet Louis outside Guy's Hospital. My sister, Diane, was already with Mum. I brought Joshua with me because she was helpless and wouldn't be able to harm any of us. We all walked into the ward. I wasn't coping too well – my anxiety hit the roof and I didn't really know what to do apart from put one foot in front of the other. I wondered whether seeing her would make my flashbacks worse, or better.

I spotted her straight away. One side of her face had collapsed, with dribble running down. Her eye was dragged down and weeping. The other side of her body was fine.

All three siblings were struck dumb. We didn't know what to say or do from our own perspective. We had had to survive around Mum and now she was as helpless as a kitten. Joshua broke the ice for us. He asked her "What's happened to your face?"

Mum gurgled "I'm not well son. And what's your name?"

"Joshua".

"Joshua. That's a nice name, and how old are you?"

"Seven".

"Seven. You're a big boy for seven. You are tall".

And so it went on. She tried to smile at me but couldn't. My heart clutched. I saw that flicker in her eye.

For a few treasured moments she was Grandma and I was her daughter, who she was close to. She was proud of me. And then it all went away. Whilst Joshua was chatting, Louis and I went to talk to the staff nurse who told us that Mum was making good progress. Even though she looked awful she would regain some kind of mobility and she would be able to walk again. And Mum being Mum, she did just that. She was back on her feet again within months of her stroke.

CHAPTER 15

THE BLACK VELVET WINTER OF JUPITER

When the hands of fate strike, it seems that it does so in one big hit after another. Never was this more apparent with Louis. His best friend of many years, Andrew, whom he had known since he was 12, was dying. Andrew's Mum, Nikki, had saved Louis from Mum's abuse as much as she could by allowing him to stay with them in Camberwell.

Andrew was one of the nicest people you could ever wish to meet. He was loved by everyone he came into contact with. And that went without saying with Louis and Andrew. As children, they were inseparable. Andrew helped Louis get his first job. His family are Cypriot and on any occasions, be they weddings, birthdays or other celebrations, Louis was included in everything.

Now Andrew was in hospital fighting for his life. He had a disease which was attacking his heart. And the only way to save him was with a heart and lung transplant. Poor Nikki – Andrew was her only son. It had only been Andrew and her for a long time. She had married Andrew's Father but he had walked out very early in their marriage, leaving Nikki to raise their son on her own. Nikki was with Andrew every minute of the day; she lived at Guy's Hospital and very rarely left his side.

Then, in the February, Andrew sadly died. His funeral was heart-wrenching. Hundreds of people attended. Louis was grief stricken. Our Mother had recovered and attended as well, crying her heart out.

It was a day of mixed emotions. Seeing my Mother and then looking at Nikki crying so many tears; I thought she would collapse when Andrew's coffin was lowered into the ground. I couldn't take my eyes off Nikki. How ever was she going to live without Andrew?

But Andrew wasn't going to remain silent for long. I thought about him for months after he passed over. I talked to him a lot believing he was in a safe and divine place where God and the Angels reside. I knew without any doubt that Andrew was most high. I promised him that I would try and always look after Nikki as best I could. As I wished him 'goodnight' I drifted off to sleep and Andrew stepped into my dreams. He looked so well. He was wearing a dark navy suit, with a red and blue paisley tie. His eyes shone and his skin colour was radiant. He didn't look emaciated as he had done in hospital. He held his hands out and grabbed my arm and took me on a journey through the clouds and high into the sky. We whizzed past the sun and landed on a beautiful island.

"This is Cyprus. This is my home. Tell Mum I'm here", he smiled.

He then took me to an apartment which overlooked the sea. It had a balcony and Andrew said "Come on Jaz, let's sit outside". We sat at a long table, and across from it, Nikki was waving and smiling at us both. She looked beautiful. Her hair was long and her face didn't have a shred of grief in it. Andrew repeated "Tell Mum I'm okay. Now you can wake up and tell her".

And that is exactly what I did. I ran down the stairs, phoned Nikki and told her exactly what I had dreamt. Nikki asked "Did you see Andrew in his coffin?"

"No Nikki, I didn't".

"The clothes you describe in your dream are the clothes I dressed him in for his coffin".

Nikki was naturally upset. But happy to know that he was well again and okay. Andrew wasn't' quite finished with me yet. And the proof that he gave me to pass on to Nikki was truly remarkable.

Later on that year, in the October, I was going to visit Cyprus for the first time. I hadn't flown for years and the thought of going on a plane was scaring me stupid. So I asked Andrew to protect us and give us a safe flight. Nikki had always said that Andrew loved Cyprus. And whenever it was time to return to England, Andrew would cry. Nikki came from the northern part of Cyprus and had had to flee for her life when her village became occupied by the Turkish.

We landed at Larnaka Airport and got a taxi to the apartments. My friend Carmel, who travelled with Josh and me had booked the apartment through a good friend of hers, Rose, who had lived in Cyprus for thirty years.

We got to the apartment in the dead of night so I couldn't see the name of where we were staying. In my mind I had talked to Andrew and promised him that I would light a candle for him at the nearest church and thank him for our safe journey. As soon as I woke up, I bathed, got dressed and walked around the outside of the apartment to find the nearest church. And there – way up high perched on a steep hill, was the smallest church that I had ever seen. Every step I took I was moaning at Andrew, telling him he could have found a church at ground level. I could hear him laughing, "Just get up there and stop moaning!"

Finally I walked into the church and it was worth every step. It was even smaller inside. It had a few pews and a beautiful altar. I lit a candle for Andrew and Nikki, and stayed there for a while, soaking up the atmosphere before walking back into the Cyprus weather.

Outside there was a tree with hundreds of brightly coloured ribbons tied to it. The song "Tie A Yellow Ribbon Round The Old Oak Tree" came to my mind. Corny I know, but it's the truth. I looked over at the apartments and saw in bold blue letters 'Andreas Apartments'. That is Andrew's name in Cypriot. I stared at that name for a long time. And then I cried and said "Well done Andy, you did good".

As soon as I got home from Cyprus I phoned Nikki and told her about the apartment's name, and the church that I had visited. I wanted Nikki to know just how much Andrew was still around. Nikki's best friends are the caretakers of the church he had taken me to. Out of all the hundreds of churches, Andrew had chosen the only one that meant that his Mum would know just how much he would always love and be there for her.

CHAPTER 16

FORGOTTEN RAINBOWS

Joshua was loving his new school. He was stretching his mind and coming home absolutely exhausted.

The school was in Purley, and every time I visited, it reminded me of Coulsdon, which was just around the corner – the little village I grew up in.

The air was different from South Norwood. Clearer and fresher, just as I remembered it. Pigeons come home to roost and that is what I wanted to do. I found a beautiful two-bedroomed house (from the outside) in Whyteleafe. However, inside I felt uneasy.

Ignoring my instincts and letting my ego take over, I went headlong into trouble. I wanted to be out of South Norwood. And this was so close to Joshua's school. Besides, maybe by moving it would help with the flashbacks of my Mother. They were not occurring as often but they were still there. Sometimes it took me to the depths of despair, but at other times it loosened its grip. I hadn't seen my Father for a while. Everything was all up in the air. And the only time I was grounded was with Joshua. He was having a happy childhood and that to me was the best thing I had achieved in my entire life. He might have sensed something from me, but I tried my best to keep the sorrow from him. I read to him a lot. I loved the bones of him. He was easy living.

It was the past that haunted me. All the while Bob kept on telling me that the answers lay within me. Sometimes I would lose my patience with him. "Bollocks Bob! You haven't got a body! Telling me the answers lie within? You see things so differently Bob. Everything is *not* all sunshine and flowers!"

"Don't you think I know that child? I have been on the Earth Plain. It is hard for a reason. It is school. Earth's school. Sometimes through your own efforts you might not seem to get even a little reward, and then maybe a few months or many years later the debt is paid. The gift is given. Always be patient. Everything has a balance. Take your time and enjoy every step of the way. Life soon ends".

CHAPTER 17

BE STILL MY LOVE, BE STILL

Because Joshua was in private school, I needed some extra money. And I needed it fast. The readings once again were helping me out and putting food on the table at least. There was no dancing around the table with hunger. It was important that I had some money squirreled away. A friend of mine came to the rescue. She worked at an agency that looked after old people in their own homes and she said that I could choose the hours I worked. All I had to do was make them a cup of tea in the afternoon or prepare them a meal. How hard could it be?

My first charge was Fred. He lived on his own and he needed his lunch made and a vacuum round the house once a week. The agency said if I wanted I could have some more work. But for now I just wanted to work for Fred. I dropped Joshua off at school and set off. I managed to find his house easily as it was round the corner from where I used to live in South Norwood. I got out of the car and walked down the path and before I could ring the bell, someone was already ringing it for me. There was a woman with her finger pressed on it. I knew she was dead but I was paralysed with fear, not because I was seeing her. It was the bell. How the hell was I going to explain to Fred it wasn't me?

I said in my mind "What's the problem? Could you please stop ringing the doorbell".

She did a double take and whispered "You can hear me?"

"Just about. Look, take your finger off the doorbell and let me see what I can do for you".

Just as she lifted her finger off, Fred answered the door. I looked at her and said "Thanks very much, now he thinks it's me that's two sandwiches short of a picnic".

She laughed. "I don't care. I just want to tell Fred I am still here".

Poor Fred. He looked absolutely petrified. I offered my hand and said "Hello. My name is Jassmine. You're expecting me?"

"I'm not deaf Love. You didn't have to ring the bell that much".

I glared at the woman and walked into the house. Fred went into the back room and sat down, putting his walking stick to one side. The spirit woman was sitting opposite him with love in her eyes. I noticed photographs of the woman standing next to Fred. I looked back at the woman who said "I'm his wife. I've just gone and I want to tell Fred that I'm still here, and I'm all right. Then I'll be happy. If you don't do it, I will ring the doorbell again!"

I couldn't quite believe what I was hearing. "No way am I going to tell your poor husband who is traumatised already by all your persistent bell ringing. My answer is No!"

She stood up, walked out of the room and rang the doorbell. "Do you want me to get that Fred?" I asked.

"No, you're all right Love. I'll get it".

He slowly walked to the door and opened it. And there she was, her finger pressed on the bell, staring at it, pushing it with all her strength.

"There's no one there", puzzled Fred.

"Have you had trouble with the doorbell before?" I asked.

"No Love, it's a mystery to me".

His wife had run out of energy and stopped ringing. She told me "My name is Pat".

I replied unenthusiastically "Hello Pat".

She smiled. She knew she had pushed me too far. Fred went back to his chair. He looked so forlorn. He wore a flat cap and a blue cardigan. He had the bluest of blue eyes and behind them there was intelligence and kindness. I looked at the photographs on the sideboard and asked "Is that your wife Fred?"

He began to cry. "Yes, that's my Pat. I lost her only a few weeks ago. I'm lost without her".

I looked at Pat, who was also crying. She didn't mean any harm. She just wanted to tell Fred she was all right. My heart went out to them both. "Would you like a nice cup of tea?"

He nodded through his tears. "Will you be all right Love? You don't know where everything is".

"I'll find my way around Fred, don't worry".

The kitchen was as neat as a pin. The cupboards were spotless and the cooker was shiny and clean. Pat kept a good house. I came back with Fred's tea, went back to the kitchen and cooked his lunch. Pat followed me and asked "Do you promise you will say something?"

I looked at her properly for the first time. She was small and plump and she was wearing a pink cardigan. She folded her arms across her chest.

I promised. "Yes Pat, you have my word". Then I served Fred his lunch.

Over the months I was able to tell Fred little things about Pat. They had a lovely garden and I often took Fred out there to sit in it and get some fresh air. Pat used to tag along too. She'd point out the flowers she had planted. She'd say "See all those Daffs in the corner? I planted them".

I would ask Fred "Did Pat plant those Daffodils?"

"Yes Love. How did you know that?"

"Lucky guess Fred".

He would smile and walk slowly around the garden with tears in his eyes. Pat stood next to him, smiling; wishing Fred could see her. This was a love that not even death could break.

CHAPTER 18

CHASING THE MORNING

Between the readings, taking Joshua to school and doing the care work, I was exhausted.

However, the home we had moved into was beautiful. It had been finished to a high specification, down to the sunken bath. But … there was something walking around … and it was something I didn't like. Sometimes when I put the key in the door, a spirit would walk through me and up the stairs. It was a masculine energy that wasn't nice. I got a friend of mine, Emma, a fantastic artist, to draw a picture of a Native American on my bedroom wall to protect the house. He was a fine looking Native, with long hair and large gold earrings. His eyes would follow you around. I thought that was a good idea as the man spirit would know that if he was roaming around the house he was still being watched.

My bedroom had an en-suite bathroom which Joshua always used. One day I asked Joshua "Why do you always run like someone is chasing you?"

He looked at me and said "Mum, I'm not frightened but that man keeps staring at me when I walk past him".

"What? The picture of the Native American? He won't hurt you Josh".

"I know but it is when he turns his head and his mouth starts to move. I can't understand what he's trying to tell me".

After nearly falling into the kitchen sink, I recovered enough to say "All right son. I see your point!"

As for the strange spirit man, I didn't want to talk to him. I felt he was bad.

CHAPTER 19

YOUR FATHER WILL TELL YOU
WHEN HE COMES HOME

Dad. I hadn't seen him for a time. It wasn't that I didn't want to see him; we just didn't see eye to eye. We were too much alike.

Guilt wears many disguises and hats, and Dad's way of coping was with sarcastic comments and a feigned disinterest that I could see right through; I couldn't fight with him. Why should I try so hard to be loved by my Father?

Because we were telepathic, connected spiritually, two souls trying to work out our differences in Earth school, he always pulled me to him by sending me his dreams. We would play catch-up with one another and I would know exactly what was going on in his life. I hadn't seen him for a few years so when he came to me in my dreams I wasn't too surprised. It was about time. His visit was long overdue.

I found myself floating outside his house. I walked through the front door and as I did so, I could hear him crying. He was wearing a dark navy blue jumper. Tears streamed down his face and he could barely catch his breath. The house still looked the same but there was something missing. Ruth. And as I woke up I realised that Ruth had passed over a few weeks ago. The next morning I dialled Dad's number. He answered "Hello?"

"Hi Dad, it's Jaz, how are you?"

"You know, don't you?"

"Know what?"

"That Ruth died a few weeks ago. She dropped down dead of a heart attack in Tooting High Street".

"I'm sorry Dad. I'll come over".

When I arrived, Dad was sitting in the same corner of the room, wearing a navy blue jumper and sobbing into his handkerchief, exactly as I had seen in my dream. Poor Dad, he was beside himself. He and Ruth had known each other for fifty years or more. I sat opposite Dad and just let him cry. I didn't know what to say. I had never seen him so vulnerable. This allowed me to get a little closer to him; his guard had come crashing down. I could try once again to form some kind of relationship with him.

It lasted for a few months but, as he got better, he became horrible. The guilt mask was put back on. The glares were back, and he was being rude, belligerent, critical and sniping. He wouldn't allow me to finish my sentences. He was putting me down, every which way.

One day I snapped. He was barking orders at me and doing me down. I took into consideration his grief but I couldn't cope. I was his daughter and he should look at me as the best thing since sliced bread. Instead, he was rude.

I shouted "Why should I do things for you? Cook and clean when you are being so rude!"

"Why not? You are my daughter. You have to do it".

"I'm your daughter *now*, huh Dad?"

"What do you want from me?" he shouted.

"Nothing!" I screamed and slammed the door. If he didn't want to get to know me, it was his loss. He had just given up an amazing child.

CHAPTER 20

LITTLE VOICE

Singing is my passion. I used to sing a lot before Joshua was born. And now I wanted to take it up again. I love jazz and blues. And now I had an opportunity to go to North London and work with a producer. The only thing was my throat was killing me and I was due to sing in the studio the next day. I hoped an early night and sleep would do the trick.

My head was thumping and my throat had razorblades dancing around my tonsils. Joshua went to bed quite early and I followed soon after with a kettle of water and lots of lemons. After plucking up the courage to swallow, sleep was a welcome pain relief.

I was woken some time later by a stranger – a very old Native American. He had long grey hair and his old skin was scored with deep lines. His eyes were closed and in one of his hands he held what looked like a baby's rattle made from wood. He shook it and then his eyes opened and then looked up and down my body as if he were searching for something. His eyes fixed on my throat. He held out his hand and said in a voice as old as time "Come with me".

I floated out of my body and saw it lying in a heap on the bed.

"Don't be afraid, Child".

We walked out of my bedroom and began to walk down a corridor which had bright turquoise walls. We started to move at speed. It felt good. We then began to slow down and stopped outside a door. The man opened it and we both walked in. There was a table in the middle of the room with two chairs. He beckoned me to sit opposite him and a silver bowl appeared in the middle of the table. The man got up and gently placed his hands on my shoulders. Without warning, he grabbed my throat and would not let go. I tore at his fingers trying to prise them away but he took no notice. His hands were getting warmer, then hotter.

Then something worse happened. I began to feel as sick as a dog. Bile rose into my mouth and then it came, brown liquid gushed out of me and into the silver bowl. It was putrid. I couldn't catch my breath. It was like one of those comedy sketches where someone projectile vomits on to the person in front of them. Finally the vomiting ceased and I began to feel much better; then fatigue overwhelmed me and I began to fall asleep.

The man finally released his grip and helped me up from the chair. We walked back to my bedroom and he gently eased me back into my body. I thanked him for healing my throat and he bade me goodbye.

I woke the next morning feeling fantastic. I jumped out of bed forgetting that I had ever had a sore throat. I tested my voice and it appeared fine. I worked for hours in the studio that day without any hitches.

CHAPTER 21

JET

The readings that I was doing were slowly improving. Now, thanks to Bob's advice to give up smoking, the messages were becoming clearer.

He was still urging me to see my Mother, but I didn't know how to walk into her house and have a showdown with her. At this moment, what good would it do? That's how I felt now. Maybe things would change.

The phone rang and broke my train of thought. The usual questions were answered, who recommended you to me, name and telephone number. And as I was speaking to the woman, as so often happens, a spirit (connected to that person) jumped in and wanted to talk before the reading. As I put the phone down there stood the most handsome spirit I had ever seen. He looked like a male model. Jet black hair swept off his face with piercing blue-green eyes, he told me he would see me when Tasha came for her reading. He then faded away. I was intrigued.

Finally Tasha arrived, followed her model man. We talked and then started the reading. He stepped forward and asked me if I would tell Tasha he was there. I did so, and she confirmed who he was. It was her boyfriend Graham, who was a troubled soul. He had taken some drugs, and although he had not intended to commit suicide, he had overdosed and found himself in the spirit world. He told me he was found face down in the bedroom and there was an ironed white shirt hanging on the wardrobe door as he was intending to go out that night.

He was telling Tasha how sorry he was to leave her and their four year old son, Ian. He was becoming agitated – he wasn't at peace. Tasha had heard Graham walking up the stairs of her house, and Ian had seen him on numerous occasions. Tasha confirmed this was true.

I asked Graham to calm down; he said "no" and walked through me. It was an uncomfortable feeling – pins and needles shot through my body, electric shocks scratched at my skin.

I shouted at him in my mind "Don't you ever do that to me again!" He looked upset and apologised. He broke down in tears and said that all he wanted to do was to tell Tasha that he will always be around. I told Graham to find peace in his soul. He replied he would never leave Tasha and Ian's side until they both passed over. I told him he would have to wait a very long time. He reminded me of Heathcliff but in reverse.

He said "I don't care." Now this was not good. Because Graham was confused and all over the place, he wasn't settled in death. He was so young – in his 30s and vibrant. He had taken the angst into his heart; I asked Bob to help him and Bob told me that his guide was trying to show him the way, light his path with loving thoughts. To help Graham go to where he was supposed to took three years.

However, some people don't always find peace when they go over; they need a lot of healing and guidance. Angels surround these troubled souls and they are counselled. They have to change the way they think about themselves, how they love their souls, and others. Some think they have unfinished business, but they really need to let go.

Another troubled man comes to mind who also found it hard to let go. His name was Declan.

CHAPTER 22

AN AFFAIR TO REMEMBER

Lin phoned me to say that a friend of hers, Amy, was having trouble with her dead husband, Declan, who was banging walls at their home and appearing and disappearing in front of her. Lin wouldn't tell me why he was feeling upset. She wanted me to tune in to find out what was wrong with him. I went to Lin's house and sat down quietly after the usual greetings. We tuned in. Her guide, One Feather, a Native American – a stick thin handsome man, who had died in his prime in battle – was standing behind her ready to help.

We both closed our eyes but it seemed that the airwaves were silent. Wherever Declan was in the ether, he certainly wasn't willing to talk to anyone. Then the silent atmosphere was broken by complete chaos. I heard a man shouting "Fucking arsehole!" and then … nothing.

I asked Bob if he could help Declan come forward; Bob said several people were trying to get him to calm down. But Declan was too angry to be talked into communication. Once again I heard "Fucking arsehole!"

I said "Declan, there is no point in swearing. Why don't you just calm down and explain what is going on. Maybe I can help you".

"He's a fucking arsehole and if I wasn't here, I would fucking kill him!"

"And if you are going to keep swearing, I will not talk to you!" I told him.

He turned his back on me, pulled his trousers down and showed me his behind. I told Lin what was going on and she laughed and said that was typical of him – a man of few words who preferred to hit out and talk later. I said "Listen Dec, if you swear, expose yourself and make me feel sick any more I will not be talking to you any time soon!" I hoped this would get through to him. He went quiet.

Lin told me he was found dead outside his local pub.

Still getting the silent treatment from Declan I was about to give up when Bob gave me an idea. Some people love to talk about their illnesses when on Earth and things don't change much when they enter the spirit world. They get hung up on their death and keep going over it. It is typical of human nature if you think about it. So I asked Declan how he passed.

Everything was quiet. Then I heard him say "I went to the Horseshoe for a few pints, and on my way home I slipped on a raised pavement. I had my hands in my pockets and couldn't stop myself from falling on my face. That's when I smashed my head on the pavement, shunting my brain. I woke up in the spirit world, and that's when I found out ..." Silence.

"Found out about what, Declan?"

"About him. My so-called friend was banging my missus! And he's mended the fence in my back garden!"

Poor Declan. He had found out the hard way that his wife was having an affair with his friend.

I could feel Declan's anger drain away and, in its place, a sense of despair and hurt pulsated from his soul.

Lin knew Declan well and he was ready to talk to her; between us he was prepared to get some help in the spirit world. He still loved Amy and told us to pass on that message to her. He understood why she had had the affair but it was such a shock to find out about her after his death. He apologised for being so angry at the beginning of the reading and blew me a kiss as he walked into the spirit world.

CHAPTER 23

NOVEMBER IN THE RAIN

Bob was trying to talk to me about my Father. He said that he couldn't cope with his guilt about never being there for me. He is a very proud man and didn't know how to love me. I said to Bob that it was easy to love my son Joshua but Bob said this was different.

"Some can give love to their children without hesitation. And others can't. Your Father and you are very similar. You're both opinionated and both think that you are right. If one of you doesn't come off your high horse sooner or later, one day it may be too late".

I knew it was down to me to mend some fences. Really, in my heart of hearts I struggled with this, but I had to answer to the wisdom of my intuition. I had a silent unseen bond with my Father.

I made him some lunch and made my way over to his home. I rang the doorbell. I heard him walk to the door, leaning on his walking stick, his bad leg unable to bend due to an operation that went wrong a few years ago. He should never have had surgery because he has full Sickle Cell Anaemia.

[Sickle Cell Anaemia is a condition where the red blood cells are crescent shaped instead of disc shaped. Disc shaped cells can move freely through blood vessels carrying an iron rich protein called haemoglobin. This also carries oxygen from the lungs to the rest of the body. Sickle cells contain abnormal haemoglobin called sickle haemoglobin. They are stiff and sticky and block blood flow in the blood vessels of limbs and organs; this can cause pain, serious infections and organ damage. I am a carrier.

My Father had been a full blown Sickle Cell sufferer for all his life but was not diagnosed until his late seventies. He coped with the pain through smoking weed. By getting out of his skull he could control it. He never complained of his pain but he must have been in agony which made him short-tempered.

Unfortunately the UK is rather behind in the treatment of Sickle Cell. America is way ahead of the game. As mentioned, I am a carrier and have inherited the trait. The trait is when there is a mix of crescent shaped cells with normal shaped cells. It is said that this condition greatly reduces the spread of malaria.]

I knew Dad would be outspoken today and that it would be a gem. He sat down and I went to the kitchen to heat up lunch. When I had served it, we sat in comfortable silence. This was one thing we did well. We had a natural telepathy. We communicated using our own secret language. We had done this since I remembered him looking at me in my incubator. Dad broke the silence. "Where's Joshua"?

"He's gone to his friend's for the day".

Dad looked me in the eye. He knew it was horse shit. I just didn't want to bring him because I wanted to see what kind of mood my Father was in first. He smiled and tutted, but he was pissed off. He loved seeing his grandson. I put the television on and watched Dad eating his lunch. He thoroughly enjoyed it and nearly licked the pattern off the plate. He then folded his arms across his chest.

"Was that okay?" I asked.

"It was all right".

I raised my eyes and smiled. He caught my expression. He pursed his lips and stretched his legs out underneath the table.

Then he produced his gem. "Why are you here? You know that when I die the house will be yours. And you will get all the money".

My jaw dropped to the floor. "Is that what you think this is all about?"

"Yes".

I stood up and stared into my Father's face. "Bye Dad".

He laughed. "See yourself out".

I got in the car and cried and cried. Tears of anger splashed on to the steering wheel of the car. I shouted into the silence "Thanks Bob".

I could feel the presence of my paternal Grandmother, Miss Lou. Even though I had never met her on the Earth, she was very much around in spirit. I have her wedding ring and always wore it when I saw Dad. She said "He's a stubborn old fool and soon he's going to see what he's done, keep showing your love to him. Try not to be angry. You'll see; things will turn around".

The cars behind me were hooting at me to drive on. I hadn't noticed that the traffic lights had changed from red to green.

CHAPTER 24

DISTINCTION DISTINCTION

Joshua was doing extremely well at school. He was learning more about nature and his surroundings. He was also learning about the arts. It was great. There were only ten children in each class and the teachers could have been sent from Heaven.

At the end of the summer term there was an awards ceremony. This was a big deal amongst the parents, and competition was rife. Many of them turned up with cameras on tripods.

I had never missed anything Joshua did at school. I just about made the event due to work, and arrived hot and sweaty; I had a nervous tick in my eye and cheek that would not go. I kept rubbing my eye in the hope that it would stop.

I compared myself to the other parents who worked themselves into oblivion; they were dishevelled and tired working two or three jobs to keep their kids in this great school.

It was time for Joshua's house to receive their awards. For English, Joshua got a Distinction. For Maths - Distinction. English Literature – Distinction. Music – Distinction. In just about all subjects Joshua got top marks. By the end of the awards I was on my feet clapping and cheering. My heart burst with pride. A parent came over and congratulated me.

I hugged Joshua tight and we walked to our battered car that was held together with sticky tape, and a wing and a prayer, while the more opulent drove away in their giant trucks. I thought to myself it's okay because my child has the brains to buy one of those cars one day.

CHAPTER 25

FALL FROM GRACE

Dad had taken a fall and the hospital rang to see whether I would pick him up and take him home. I felt like saying "Just shoot him out of a cannon" but instead I said "That's fine. I'll pick him up".

Dad had a carer but had fallen in the small hours of the morning. He had the good sense to touch his alarm medallion and an ambulance arrived. Dad was becoming more unsteady on his feet; on this occasion he had gone to sit down and missed the chair by inches. He was more shaken than hurt and had been taken to hospital as a precaution.

I walked into St George's Hospital, Tooting, London and found him. By the expression on his face he looked as if he were ready to be discharged. He looked pissed off. He had been stuffed into a wheelchair, his knees practically around his ears. When he saw me, he couldn't help but smile. Then his mask went up. It made my heart dance. "It doesn't take much to love me, Dad", I thought.

'How am I going to put this man, who is well over six feet tall, into my car?' I wondered. His left leg would not bend. I wheeled him to my car; the wheelchair was like a shopping trolley which went in all directions except the one I needed to go in! It was getting dark and Dad was getting cold. I pushed the passenger seat back as far as it would go and managed to poke and prod him in.

He swore profusely, telling me how everyone else found it easy to put him in their car. I snapped "And where the fuck are they now?" That shut him up. I had an image of me beating him with his walking stick. He caught my thoughts and held on to it more tightly. It made us both laugh.

"Thanks dear".

"That's okay".

We drove home without any further hassle. I pulled up outside his house and dragged Dad out of the car and managed to walk him up the path, get him through the door and settle him in front of the gas fire in the back room. He told me he was hungry so I nipped across the road and got him some fish and chips. Not an ideal dinner but it would have to do. He literally inhaled the food and then settled down. I sat opposite him and promptly fell asleep.

When I woke, he had put some keys on the table. "You better get home, you look tired. Here, take these keys to the house".

I yawned, stretched and put them in my pocket. "Okay Dad, I'll speak to you tomorrow". I kissed the top of his head and took the hour long journey home. As I drifted off to sleep that night, my Grandmother was blowing me a kiss 'goodnight'.

CHAPTER 26

BENNY BOY

Ben was a man who I had never met. He was a proud, 'salt of the Earth', 'what you see is what you get' type. He didn't mince his words and would turn the air blue if he felt like it. His home was his castle, where he looked after his son and daughter.

His daughter, Chris, is a chip of the old block. Over the years she has shocked me to my shoes with her outspoken spirit but also made me laugh out loud. She never backs down from anything. Saying that, she is easily hurt and very sensitive.

I had given Chris a reading and had some messages to give to her Father from her Mother who had passed a few years before. Ben had confirmed some of the evidence that Chris had told him. He said "Even though I am a bit of a sceptic, if there is an afterlife, the only person I will contact when I'm gone will be Jassmine". Chris told me about his promise.

When Ben had said this, he was well. But as the months passed, Ben became ill. There was something wrong with his stomach, and was having tests as he was rapidly losing weight. His skin became sallow and pallid. Poor Chris. She didn't know what to do to help her dad. All she knew was that she didn't want him to suffer. And this was where Chris' forthright personality was going to test me. What was wrong with him; and did he have to suffer? Because she couldn't bear to see him in such pain.

I am not God so I didn't feel it was my place to tell her even though she was begging me to. I was lying exhausted on my bed with my ear against the receiver. I didn't want to answer her, because experience has taught me not to give people too much information as clients can sometimes get freaked out – they can't take it all in.

I closed my eyes and sensed Chris' Mum hovering near me. She said "Tell her, love. She will feel better knowing about her dad. Tell her. She will be worse if she doesn't know".

Chris was crying by this time. Her Mum showed me two lumps in his stomach. It didn't look good; they would have to be operated on. And Ben didn't have long. I couldn't see him living beyond September and this was July. He had already survived one year and he was exhausted.

Chris and her Mum were still trying to persuade me so, with my heels dragging behind me, I told her "I can't see Ben living beyond September. He's got two lumps in his stomach. It's not good, Chris".

Chris breathed a sigh of relief; she felt better already. She rolled her sleeves up and nursed her dad at home. She took to sleeping in a chair near him so she could keep an eye on him. One morning, in September, as she awoke, she saw Ben leave his body. He walked towards her, cupped her face with his hands and said "You know I don't want to leave you, but I'm very tired. I need to go. I love you very much".

He then returned to his body, and as he did he took a deep breath. A few days later, he passed over. This is when I nicknamed him 'Benny Boy'. He came to Chris through a few readings but the first time he came to me personally was when I was sitting in his old car. Chris had kindly given me his six seater blue Daihatsu HiJet. I loved that car. It was great. I had seen more spirits sitting in the empty seats than any humans that ever sat there. Joshua's friends would pile in and they loved the way the car bounced around the country lanes.

On this particular day I was travelling home when another car cut me up, nearly causing me to crash. I heard a man's voice shout from the passenger seat "You fucking wanker!" I slammed on the brakes and looked round. There was a man wearing a flat cap, white shirt and dark trousers; he had beautiful skin and eyes. It was Ben and it appeared he wanted to travel a mile or two in the car that he had loved. He had been exactly the same when Chris drove. It was so funny. He now accompanies me when I am afraid or not too sure of things. I can hear him saying "Take no notice of that git! I'll sort him out." And somehow the situation is resolved. He's my lovely spiritual Dad – a Fearless Fred with a twinkle in his eye.

CHAPTER 27

CHEF

Joshua wanted a dog. He started by asking then, as children do, he started begging. To put him off I said that the dog would be sent to him. Famous last words.

Whilst standing outside Joshua's school waiting for him to come out, I could see out of the corner of my eye a black and white fluff ball scampering around a woman who could barely keep him under control. I caught the dog's eye, and his large ears pricked up; he then dragged the woman across the road, sat next to me and looked up at me as if to say "What took you so long? When are you going to look after me? You know we belong together. "

The woman apologised and said he had never done that before. "I don't know what's got into him".

I thought to myself "I know what's got into him. He's telling me he belongs to me".

And from then on, I kept bumping into this black and white powder puff. He looked so strange, like a cartoon. He is a cross Staffordshire Bull Terrier-Border Collie. He has the head, legs and close fur of a Staffie, but the snout and long body of a Collie. One day I found myself looking out of my kitchen window and there he was, walking past my house. He looked at me and leapt over a brick wall to try and get to me – barking and wagging his tail.

Another day I bumped into his owner, Laureyn, and complimented her dog. She told me he was a bit of a handful. I asked his name and she told me it was Chef. I found myself asking if I could walk him one day and she replied "I don't see why not".

Laureyn lived around the corner, so the following day Joshua and I took Chef over Farthing Downs, a beautiful wooded area with acres of land – plenty of ground for Chef to cover and wear him out. But first I had to walk him on the lead which he hated. He shook his head violently, trying to get his head out of his collar and he managed it. I ended up rugby tackling him to the ground. It was that or watch him go under a double-decker bus. I slipped his collar back on and we set out again. Chef leapt up to my shoulder and on the way down he caught my arm and sank his razor sharp puppy teeth into my coat sleeve, and he was not going to unhinge his jaw any time soon.

Joshua looked on with his mouth open. I said to him "So you want a dog do you?"

"Yes", he nodded his head enthusiastically.

Chef finally unlocked his jaw and dropped to the pavement which I thought was a bloody miracle as Staffies don't normally loosen their grip, even in death. Maybe the Border Collie in him decided to give me a chance.

He walked, weaving in and out of our legs. I thought "This is one crazy animal!" and fell in love with him there and then. Joshua flanked him and between us we got him to Farthing Downs, where I let him off the lead. He loved it. He ran and ran. I noticed that even at only seven months old he was humping everything, even a blade of grass.

After prising him off people's legs and their dogs I walked him away far from anything that could distract him.

But then we lost him. After making myself hoarse calling his name for three hours, we found him. A woman had managed to catch him and put him on a lead; she was waiting for us at the entrance to the Downs. Praise the Lord.

I nearly threw him back at Laureyn, went home and fell into exhausted sleep.

CHAPTER 28

FUCK NUTS - FUCK NUTS

A few days later, Laureyn came round to me in tears. She told me Chef had virtually held her family hostage with his behaviour. Incessant barking, destroying furniture, biting her children and humping everything. She asked "Would you like him?"

"Yes".

I didn't anticipate what I would have to go through, but I would do it all again.

And so Joshua got his wish. Chef has the intelligence of a Border Collie with the spirit of a Staffie (that told everyone to go swivel on a stick)! And he uses it to his advantage. He is incredibly telepathic. He also saw spirits from the readings I did at home. Whenever he saw one, his hackles would rise and his top lip curl. He looked as if he were auditioning for 'The Hound of The Baskervilles'. I would have to calm him down and put him in his bed. When he got older, he ignored the spirits. But his hormones were still raging. In dog years he was at the height of his sexual prowess, a randy teenager and his humping was getting worse. So one sunny afternoon he was neutered.

When I collected him from the vets, he was still a little drowsy from the anaesthetic and he behaved like a normal dog, walking to heel beautifully. Then, as the anaesthetic wore off, he got a second wind and bolted and even though he was hobbling and his gait was wide, he managed it. I tore after him, grabbed the scruff of his neck and growled "You little shit!", and put his lead on.

I was told it would take up to 8 months for his hormones to balance out. Try three years. Chef was his own dog. As far as he was concerned, I was his bitch. He was the alpha male and he didn't give a damn what I said to him. As soon as I took him off the lead, I would watch him disappear over the horizon, trying to run to catch up with him. I can hear you ask "Why did you let him off the lead?" Because he needed to run. The Border Collie is a working dog and a forty minute walk will not cut it;, they need two to three hours a day – I kid you not. After that they then tend to level out and calm down at home.

However, Chef's behaviour was becoming impossible. Laureyn had warned me but I thought I could turn his behaviour around. He barked and howled like a lunatic at home, and pulled on the lead as if he were hauling coals to Newcastle. And nobody could step over him– not if they valued their toes anyway.

It was like that joke: Little Red Riding Hood is walking through the woods, meets the Big Bad Wolf and says to him "My my, what big eyes you have". The Wolf says "Fuck off, I'm having a crap".

That is how I felt with Chef. He was taking the piss and it had to stop. There was one way that I had read in a dog behaviour book, and that was to ignore him when he misbehaved. So both Joshua and I blanked him.

You could see the cogs turning in Chef's brain "Okay, if you are going to ignore me I will bark even louder". And he did. He also chewed things, and destroyed his bedding. He had cotton wool balls all around his mouth and looked like a four legged Father Christmas.

The house was covered in them. I dutifully cleared it all up as Chef sat looking on, grinning from ear to ear. Yes, dogs do smile. I fed him, walked him and cleaned up his poop, everything apart from wipe his arse. By day Chef was beside himself. At night he would lay in his bed looking at me with a glint in his eye. On one occasion I was sweeping the floor with a dustpan and brush. Chef grabbed the brush, chewed the handle and pulled out the bristles. He then grabbed the pan and split it in two. I thought to myself "So I'm not cleaning the floor today".

I still ignored him. He barked and playfully growled in my ear. Out of desperation he leapt on to the windowsill, perched up there, barked some more and wagged his tail which thumped against the pane. Dribble dropped all over the floor. I snuck a look at him. His top lip had got caught up under his gum and he looked like Elvis, his white fangs on display. He looked so funny I really wanted to laugh. Instead I turned my back on him. He took a flying leap and landed on my back as I was cleaning up the remnants of the dustpan. I shook him off and walked out of the kitchen in feigned disgust. He followed me into the living room and tore around until he was worn out. "I have to tough this out", I thought. My cheek began to twitch. I turned to Bob and asked "What am I going to do?" He remained silent.

CHAPTER 29

HEAD-ON-IST-IC

Chef was calming down after my ignoring him. Thanks to Caesar Milan's TV programme and my taking control, Chef became *my* bitch.

He was still eccentric, chasing the biggest stick (or branch) that he could find and then holding it proudly in his mouth, taking out people as he walked past. It was embarrassing, although most people would see the funny side of being tripped up.

However, demanding dog or not, I still had to work. A friend of mine volunteered to walk Chef when I was busy. It was Sunday and I was off to do some readings. I told my friend to walk him anywhere but the Downs as he couldn't be around horses.

I was in the middle of a reading when everything disappeared and I could see Chef's face, surrounded by light. He was sitting with his funny back legs and boxy head, sending me a message from his mind to mine. I heard him say "Come home. My head hurts".

I finished the reading so fast it made my head spin.

I walked home as quickly as I could and there was no excited bark to greet me. I phoned my friend and asked her "Where is Chef? And what's wrong with his head?"

She started to cry and told me "I can't lie. I took him over the Downs and he saw a horse and chased it. The horse kicked him in the head; he nearly lost an eye and his life. The vet had to drive to the middle of the Downs – she saved Chef's life".

The vet had said that if Chef remembered the kick he would be hesitant to try and take on a horse again. Poor Chef – when he came home his Buster collar was all skew-whiff. He looked so sorry for himself. He had stitches over his left eye. Thank goodness for his strong Staffie head – it saved his life. He did remember that horse, and now if he is near horses, he runs to me to let me know and I put him on the lead. That makes him feel safe and all he does is duck and growl at them.

Twelve years on, he is still as mad as a March hare but I wouldn't swap him for the world.

CHAPTER 30

I SMELL CANCER

Joshua's grades were falling and I wanted to know why. I wasn't the only parent noticing as others had also commented on their children.

I asked Josh if he was happy with his teacher and said he was fine. However, the next term was the same with no improvements in grades. Josh would soon be going on to secondary school and he needed to knuckle down.

I told him I would see his teacher but he replied "Don't go and see her, Mum. She's not well". And sure enough he was right. She was diagnosed with throat cancer.

I asked Josh how he knew she was so ill, and he said "I could smell it".

I stared at him. "Okay son".

I have heard of dogs smelling illness, even sensing when someone is about to have an epileptic fit, but this was the first time I knew of a human doing this.

CHAPTER 31

PAPA'S GOT A BRAND NEW BAG

Dad was a lot better but he still seemed a little unsteady on his feet, although he hadn't fallen again. I had decided to go over and see him with Joshua.

Dad was talking to Josh like it was going out of fashion, gesticulating with his hands, just as I do to get my point across. We even have the same thumbs.

I sat back and looked on for a while, then I closed my eyes and felt my ancestors around me; Miss Lou my Grandmother, and Dad's wife Ruth. There were also others I didn't recognise.

Ruth went over to Dad and kissed him on the cheek before floating through the wall. Dad touched his face and stared into the room where once his late wife had been. The room was filled with the air of the spirits. I could almost push them and see them bob around as orbs of light.

CHAPTER 32

A BORDELLO AND A SHALLOW OVATION

Joshua was once again doing well at school. His teacher had left to start her treatment. That was not the problem. Sometimes women can be so competitive with each other. Never more so than outside the school gates. Sometimes you get a "Hello" and at other times the same person would look through you. It really pissed me off. From the time you become a parent, there are mothers saying "My baby could walk at six months old". "Well mine was reciting 'War and Peace' before pre-school". It is just ridiculous.

On this particular occasion, when I went to collect Joshua from school I was about to say 'hello' to one of the mothers when she just brushed past me.

That evening, I fell into a deep sleep on the sofa. I began to dream that I was standing outside a large castle. Looking up, I could see the turrets poking up into the clouds. There was a being standing by the door. He looked like an angel without wings. He was draped in white with light emanating from his body. I am speaking of him as masculine but I was actually unsure. He looked male until he smiled when he became feminine. His golden brown skin shimmered in the sun. |He held out his hand to invite me into the castle, which I was glad to do because the sun was beginning to burn my face. He took me through the rooms which were light and airy and then into the back garden. I heard a sound; the being said "Look" and there was a sight I would never forget. Kneeling down on little mats were some of the mothers who were arsey with me. They were dressed in designer suits. They were holding little trowels in their hands and were digging the path. They had no expression on their faces – they appeared to be in a trance.

I saw a spare mat and trowel in the corner. The being stepped closer to me and said "Do you want to join them?"

I shook my head. I didn't want to be like that.

He led me back to the front door, and there, in front of me, was the most beautiful garden I had ever seen. I gasped. It had all of my favourite flowers in it. Sunflowers, Sweetpeas, Hollyhocks, Lavender, Forget-Me-Nots and Buttercups. The being stood next to me as we both admired the vista, and told me "Now, here is *your* garden".

CHAPTER 33

THE DEVIL'S IN THE DETAIL

Decisions, decisions. When clients entered my home they would leave their vibes behind them. Sometimes they were good, but at other times it took a while to clear up the heavy atmosphere. Between Chef, Joshua and the ghosts that visited the rooms, I needed my home to be a sanctuary and not a conveyer belt of orbs with spirit faces bobbing around the kitchen.

I craved my own space and in Caterham, Surrey was a shop called the Spell Box. It sold crystals and all things related to spiritual matters. The owners, Kenny and Anthony (Tony), said they were looking for a resident reader, but needed to interview prospective applicants before making a decision. A few days later they phoned to tell me that I had got the residency. What Kenny and Tony would do was promote me to their customers.

I hired a room in the back of the shop. In time I was becoming busier and busier, and it was great meeting new people.

I also wanted to start my own spiritual circle. I felt ready and more confident in what I was being taught by Bob and the spirit world. It was a test and a half. Running circles was totally different from one-to-one readings. In a circle you have to build up the energy and help people to develop themselves and keep the circle safe. Teaching people was a different matter. In every walk of life, teaching has to be seen as a vocation. If it is not seen like that you can't teach with an open heart and allow your intuition to guide you.

That is what |I wanted to do but I was a fledgling, and baby birds fall over a lot before they can fly. I take my hat off to the late great Doris Stokes, who could fill the Albert Hall and read so well to vast amounts of people. But Doris Stokes I ain't so I entrusted the help of others who had a lot of experience. Mark, a great healer and medium; Sue Williams who had been sitting in circles for well over 30 years; Shirley Williams (no relation) an accomplished medium and healer in her own right.

Mark would sit opposite me, and Sue and Shirley would sit opposite each other when we first started. There were only a few people who attended as it was an open circle. The numbers varied considerably from week to week, which was fine; it was all in the learning. Bob stood behind me and helped to tune into people and guide them. I needed to get my mojo spiritual legs on.

The first few circles were fine and then a young man, Edward, joined us. Aged around twenty, he was quiet, pale and unassuming. He didn't look anyone in the eye but I took that for him being shy. Bob stood behind me and said "Be careful Child. He's not right". I soon found out what he meant.

The circle was going so well that new people were joining each week and asking if I could teach them the tarot cards, through which I could also teach them to use their intuition. They did this by putting their hands over one of the cards and saw what came to mind.

I ran one class during the day and another in the evening. People came from all walks of life and we practiced reading to each other; over the next few weeks we were beginning to get very good evidence of the spirit world. Not only that, but the energy was positive.

When Edward was in the class, Bob would still warn me about him. Edward didn't' seem to contribute to the classes, but that was okay because some are late starters, or shy; it takes them a while to pluck up the courage to say anything. But over a few weeks, members of the group were phoning me to tell me that they were getting bad vibes from him; they he made them feel weird. So, at the next class, I asked Edward if he needed any help with tuning in with his cards and offered to work with him.

As we connected, I began to feel negative vibes; he was dabbling in Satanism. I asked him outright and he didn't deny it. As he was talking to me, his face was deathly pale, his eyes dark and he had a demented grin on his face. It was pure evil.

Bob stood behind him and raised his tomahawk, as if he were going into battle. Edward's face kept shifting in front of me, his body appeared possessed as if evil was controlling him. A twisted face overshadowed his, laughing and mocking me. It looked half animal and half human. Its black legs were crouching at the side of Edward's, its tail was swishing around its back. It looked ready to jump; it gathered its strength ready to attach itself to me. Just as the creature was about to jump, Bob brought his axe up and struck it hard on its head, casting it out of Edward at the same time. Edward shrank back in his chair and twisted round to where Bob was standing; he could sense someone was there.

Whilst all this was going on, I was trying to calm the class down because, even though they could not see what was going on, some of the class could see grotesque faces and rings of fire around the group. One student ran out of the class. Edward started to chuckle, realising what he had done.

Bob showed me where Edward practiced negativity; half of his home was modern, and the other was very old. Bob showed me through his eyes the imposing dark walled wooden panels. He then took me upstairs to a room where stood a book full of negative material – evil symbols and demonic literature. Edward confirmed what I was being shown. I was petrified. Bob told me to close the class immediately which I did, with a prayer. I told Edward that until he was ready to give up his evil ways he was not welcome in the class.

The room needed to be cleansed with sage brush smoke. I had to bathe when I got home; I didn't feel well. This experience had taken its toll on my body. I spent the next three days in bed, virtually unable to move. Bob stood in the corner of my room waiting for me to recover; protecting me. He had his tomahawk in his hand, ready to strike out. Joshua and Chef were fed and watered, but in-between I slept. I felt like shit. Bob said that I had used all of my resources in the battle with evil that had taken over Edward's body.

I told Edward to never come back to the circle or tarot class again. After that, nobody saw him around the local area for the next few weeks as he lay low. He was conspicuous by his absence as he was distinctive; he always wore a black and white leather jacket and drove a yellow Ferrari.

All was calm once again in the classes and circle. A month later, I was ready to set out and run the spiritual circle at the Spell Box. I put my hand on the front door ready to leave when I heard Bob say "You can't go, Child. You cannot go to the circle tonight".

"Why? What's the problem? I have to go Bob, I'm running the circle tonight. I'm going!"

"You are not!" and with that I felt Bob pull me back. I felt dizzy and nauseous. I crawled back to the sofa and phoned the Spell Box and told Kenny and Anthony that I couldn't make it.

Kenny said "Everybody's here waiting for you Jaz. You can't let people down at the last minute".

I asked who was at the Circle and Anthony told me.

I suggested "Get Sue on the phone and see if she will run it for me. She has the experience and I'm sure she won't mind",

Anthony asked Sue and she agreed. As soon as I put the phone down, I felt better. "Bob!" I yelled.

Later I was told by Sue that Edward had attended the circle and people had begun to feel strange. Then all hell broke loose. The students were screaming and crying, not liking what they felt, but not understanding why. To calm them down, Sue recited the Lord's Prayer.

Edward's evil attachment enjoyed the show. Even though Bob had released one of the entities, there were many more around him. The following week Edward chanced his luck again and turned up for the circle. He didn't even get the chance to step through the door. He needed help but I wasn't equipped to deal with it, although I could point him in the right direction.

However, he wasn't even going to try, or maybe he couldn't. The forces would not let him go. I do hope he has found himself and is now walking in the light.

CHAPTER 34

GO TELL DAD

Dad was falling over more frequently and the hospital had to make sure that he was either picked up by a relative, or met at his own home by one. My brother and sister had different fathers. Dad had another daughter who lived in America, which obviously made it impossible for her to care for him, as much as she wanted to. How ironic that both my parents were in shit street with their health.

Neither of them ever anticipated that they would ever become infirm and old. In my Father's youth he had a natural arrogance and self-assurance (as youth affords most of us). With his good looks and winning smile he could have got away with murder. As it was, although he broke a lot of hearts, he was always forgiven.

He had never imagined that one day he would have to rely on his daughter, with whom he had never really connected. I wanted to run in the opposite direction but I needed this time with my Father to pour some water over my troubled soul. I could not let go; I needed to know what Dad saw. Did he see spirits and was he aware of the other world as my Mother had been?

And now, here I was, looking across the table at him watching him eat. Without thinking how to word my question, I blurted out "Dad, do you see spirits?"

He carried on eating and I held my breath, hoping he could not hear my heart beating. I wondered if he sensed how important his response would be. I didn't want him to pull the shutters over his eyes as then he would not look or talk to me. But that didn't happen. Instead he shot me a look and I knew exactly what he was thinking. Yes he could see spirits but he didn't know how to express himself without appearing vulnerable.

He took another bite of dinner and spoke. "Of course".

"Who was the last spirit you saw?"

"Ruth, I saw Ruth."

"Do you want to talk about it?"

He put his knife and fork down. "Of course. I came home from one of the boring old people's gatherings. As I left the building it was raining and I knew that I could catch a cold". (I smiled at this point – we are so similar. If I am caught in the rain for even a minute I catch a cold). He continued "I was really missing Ruth and as I put the key in the door I started to cry. I walked upstairs to the back bedroom and looked at myself in the mirror. I cried out to Ruth to help me out of my wet clothes. And then I saw her looking at me. She was standing at the bedroom door with her hands on her hips. She said to me 'Stop crying, and get out of your clothes. I am still here'. I stared at her, then we talked for a time but when I turned round to face her, she had gone".

I shook my head and looked deep into my Dad's eyes. I instantly understood he had always known about me which was why had he visited me in dreams and how we could communicate without speaking.

Nodding my head I asked him "So you have seen spirits all your life haven't you?"

"For as long as I can remember".

CHAPTER 35

VIOLET

I was still looking after Fred and his wife, Pat, was still making her presence felt. The agency asked if, while en route to Fred's, I could nip round to a woman called Violet who needed a cup of tea and a biscuit in the afternoon.

She lived in a warden assisted flat and I liked her instantly. I could see why she was named Violet as her eyes were vivid violet blue, and they twinkled with warmth and intelligence. Due to a heart condition she could not move easily and needed an oxygen cylinder to help her breathe.

We liked each other instantly and a fifteen minute chat with a cup of tea turned into half an hour. Over the afternoons I visited Violet, there was the spirit of a man in uniform standing behind her chair. His hands rested on her shoulders and when she found it difficult to breathe he stood closer. His uniform was Royal Air Force. Over the next few months he never left her side and, as Violet's health deteriorated, his energy became stronger. He was more visible to me and lighted emanated from his body. Violet had taken a turn for the worse and I knew she was on her way out. I walked up the stairs to her flat with a lump in my throat and waited outside her door for a few minutes to compose myself before letting myself in.

I called her name but, after not getting any reply, I went to her bedroom. Two nurses were present – although 'nurse' was a loose term; I was appalled at their attitude. They were gossiping about someone being pregnant. I stood at the foot of the bed and nodded a 'Hello' to Violet. The women paused for breath and grudgingly acknowledged my presence, although I had no wish to speak to them as I was furious. One told me to leave but I refused and stood my ground.

Instead I stared into Violet's eyes and knew she did not want me to leave her. Her hair was a mess so I grabbed a brush and tidied it up. One of the nurses said it wasn't necessary but I glared at her and retorted that it certainly was. Violet smiled and gasped for breath.

Her eyes told me 'Goodbye' and I nodded, my eyes full of tears. The man in uniform hovered above her head. He was not leaving his post.

Eventually an ambulance arrived. Her catheter was so full of urine that it dragged and hurt her. She winced and closed her eyes with pain but as she was wheeled away she opened them and tried to say "Goodbye". Her breathing was so laboured she was gasping for breath like a fish out of water. I waved to Violet and then ran back into the flat.

I glared at the 'nurses'. "Good job, you must be so proud of yourselves. Well done." They just stared at me and did not reply, instead going back to their gossiping.

I felt so sad as I got in the car, but then Bob ducked into my head. He was laughing and I said out loud "What is so fucking funny?"

"How many times have I taught you there is no need to be upset when someone makes their transition? Your friend is going to embark on the greatest adventure of her lifetime. She is going home. She won't suffer any more with her breathing. She will breathe without pain. You should not grieve but be happy that your friend has chosen a good day to die".

I thought about it. Violet had had no quality of life, just sitting in her flat looking at four walls, gasping for breath every time she moved. We would not let an animal suffer like that, so why should a human? My tears were selfish and Bob was right yet again. Violet wouldn't miss being trapped in her body. She passed away in the early hours of the morning.

That night, Violet came to me in a way that has never been repeated. As I fell into a deep sleep I could see an empty silver picture frame. Where the photograph should have been was a swirling mist. As the mist spread a young Violet emerged, smiling and moving effortlessly. Her hair looked beautiful – shining brown and shoulder length. Her violet eyes were shining and dancing with happiness. She was wearing a uniform and materialising next to her was the man who had not left her side since Violet was nearing death. He looked so handsome with his jet black hair swept back from his face. They made a very handsome and happy couple.

Violet's funeral was a week later. Her friends were gathered in her friend's apartment which was across from Violet's, and I had been invited. As I poked my head around the door they were reminiscing about her. One of her friends had a photo album. I knew Violet had no children so I asked if there was a photo of her husband. "Yes dear, here he is. Take a look". It was exactly the same photograph I had seen in my dream.

One of Violet's friends told me "They were inseparable but sadly Violet's husband died early on in their marriage through illness".

I smiled through my tears. At last they were reunited ... and importantly, happy.

CHAPTER 36

SANGHEETA

Sangheeta was one of the most beautiful spirits I had ever seen. Her husband, Martin, had come for a reading and as he walked into my kitchen he looked as if he was carrying the weight of the world on his shoulders.

He sat down and started to shuffle the Tarot cards; as he did so, I began to feel incredibly dizzy and sick, so much so I had to hold the table for support. I felt myself being spun around in the air and then crash into rocks in the sea, my body smashed into pieces. However in the next moment a beautiful sense of peace swept over me and I felt the presence of a woman behind me, wearing a red sari. The material gently stroked my cheek. The woman had the most beautiful face I had ever seen, her eyes the deepest brown, her skin luminous. She whispered "My name begins with S. Please tell my husband".

I opened my eyes and told Martin what I had seen. He began to cry. It was his beloved wife Sangheeta. They had been married for only one day. Sangheeta was killed in a paragliding accident. The cable had snapped and her body was smashed into ten pieces on the rocks. She still had the henna from their wedding on her hands. As you can imagine her whole family were grief stricken.

She gave me some more information about her family and it wasn't just the tragedy of the day that really hit home. It was the fact that before her wedding she had promised her sister Neelam something and it seemed that she had fulfilled that promise. Neelam had been diagnosed with throat cancer and had a large lump inside her throat. Before Sangheeta had left she told Neelam she would step into her sister's place and take the cancer away if she could.

At the same time Sangheeta had the accident, Neelam heard the doorbell ring. She thought it was strange as the apartment had an intercom system and she could only buzz people in through the main front door. However she had a bell on her own door. She peered through the spy hole and saw Sangheeta standing outside with a group of their ancestors who had passed away. Sangheeta smiled at her sister and waved. Neelam could not work it out. Why was she there? But when Neelam opened the door everyone had disappeared.

Confused she stood rooted to the spot for some time before walking back into the apartment. She sat down and went to touch her cancerous lump. But it had gone.

Later, Neelam had checks and scans but no trace of the lump was found. The doctor said it was a miracle; the medical profession had no logical explanation.

Sangheeta's spirit had kept her promise.

CHAPTER 37

THE GREEN FROG SKIN – FEBRUARY 2001

I love New York. I had fallen in love with the place when I had visited a few years ago with some DJ friends. It was magical. Every time I saw a yellow cab I smiled to myself and thought "I'm in the Big Apple!"

Revisiting her in my dreams felt good until one in particular which was very different.

I was walking down 42nd Street. It was deserted and felt like a ghost town. I looked up and even the sky was strange – it was light green. I shook my head in my dream and thought "Where are all the people?" Then I got my answer. Hundreds of people appeared out of nowhere. They were screaming and running in the opposite direction to where I was walking. The building started to shake and dust rained down on their heads. I was watching all the mayhem unfold.

As I looked on at these poor people their skin began to peel away from them. It was horrific. I once again put my head back and watched the strange coloured sky open to show the face of a huge man with sunlight for hair. His eyes were crystals. He reached down and lifted me up and away from New York. He showed me the rain forests which were on fire. He showed me people being killed in different countries in the name of religion.

"Until every religion walks through the same door there will never be peace on Earth, and these poor people will continue to suffer". He showed me New York once again and with his giant hand he drew a golden door. He pushed it open and there was a huge round table. The leaders of every religion were seated round it. Everyone sat in peace holding hands and talking. The man closed the door and placed me down into New York. He then bent forward and whispered "Now I want you to wake up and write this down".

As I woke up I could hear a gentle voice saying get a pen and paper and write this down now my child. I grabbed and pen and waited to see what was to be dictated to me. Here it is.

Soulmates

Walking up the corridor
Your coat brushed past mine
Our silver chords sparked at last into life
Thank you God

For I know that from that moment on
I would not be alone
Because I just met my soulmate of old
Of course you didn't know it was me
Who had played a part in your life
For so many centuries

Whenever I tried to look at your soul
By staring deep into your eyes
You would abruptly close the window
And what remained was a puzzled expression
That danced around your smile

Hurrying along to Nutfield Ward
(I would make any excuse to get there)
Just to catch a glimpse of you
Left my patient's notes on the desk
The best one yet I'd said that my stethoscope had gone
But you pointed to my neck and said that I still had it on

At last the Heavens opened
The cosmic masters kicked open your window
That had been so stubbornly glued shut
By long ago lost memories

The rain came down in sheets

Heaven was having a spring clean
I fumbled around in my pocket
Trying to find my car keys
I dropped them
You picked them up
I looked into your soul
At last you recognise me?
What took you so long?
My Valentines song

Oh what joy
Dance upon a Rainbow
And colour me seven
This is the bridge between Earth and Heaven
In the silence we spoke
In the sacred dead of the night
We came alive
Talking secretly about our dreams that laid gently
Inside

The hospital looked on in amazement
For only love cures all
A light band of gold ran around
My soulmate and I

We exchanged our sacred vows to one another
On a beach by the setting sun
God smiled upon His children
He felt too emotional to speak
As he joined us to make one

The Karmic masters of life's imagination
Decided to put us to the test

They thought it was best
Oh no! The band of gold
Made by time of old
You decided to go back to Heaven
To fulfil your dreams on some other time's level

No source could match the sadness and pain
We said goodbye to one another in the September rain
I leant against your casket
Pressing my heart against the wood
Oh I wish someone would take me
Oh I wish they would
I could be next to you
In that casket of an empty shell

Something caught my attention
I could hear an animal screaming in my ear
Poor thing it must be caught in a trap
For why was it screaming like that?
I looked up into the mourners' faces
And realised that I was that animal
Wailing in agony

Someone ushered me into the car
Went home and gave me a cup of tea
"There now, you'll feel better" she said
"No I won't. I'd be better off dead"

Months crept past not daring to speak
Years flew by during one week
Then one summer's day feeling lonely as usual
You appeared by my side in a shadow of light
Looking straight at me, you smiled with delight

You spoke telepathically and you said

"The band of gold has temporarily been separated
But my life and love for you has been elevated
No more tears you will cry
The love of my life, the apple of my third eye

The Karmic masters have a mission for you
That's why I have been sent away for now
Because you've got a lot to do
When the mission has been completed
And the eagle has landed
I'm allowed to take your hand
So that we can go and visit some faraway land
But until then my friend
My apple pie Valentines heart's content
I have to take the other half of the ring
And wait for you
For some other time's spring

The circle of life
Life is a circle
For when the band of gold is conjoined once again
We can go and dance in the rain
On a rainbow
Because circles are round
Circles are whole
The rainbow of life is old
It is whole
So when we meet again
The circle will begin
The love of my life
My Valentine's friend"

CHAPTER 38

MADAME KOTO

My Mother had decided to leave Peckham and move to somewhere in Croydon, Surrey. I live close to Croydon and quite frankly having my Mother living too near to me freaked me out. Why she'd chosen to leave Peckham where she had lived for well over forty years was a mystery to me and one I didn't care or dare to solve. Peckham was Mother's 'manor'. She had friends there that she had known back home in Jamaica.

My brother Louis would not tell me which road she was living in because he said it wouldn't have done me any good to know. He was protecting me as he always did. To be honest with you, it made me feel worse not knowing. But Louis refused to tell me and this is where the spirit world stepped in.

I was due to do a reading at my home and the client was just ringing the doorbell when the phone started to ring. It's like you say to yourself "Do I leap on the phone to see who's calling, or should I be professional and let the person in?"

I ignored the phone and sat the woman down at my kitchen table. When I did readings at home I would never unplug the phone or have it on silent because if there was a client with whom I didn't feel safe, I could use the excuse of answering the phone. Silly really because if someone wanted to hurt me they wouldn't wait for me to pick up the phone and call the police; however, knowing it was there made me feel secure.

The phone kept ringing so I asked the lady to shuffle the cards while I answered it. It was Andrew's Mum Nikki. She asked me if I knew were Mum was as she hadn't heard from her. I replied I heard she was living in Yorkshire Square but I didn't know the house number.

Then something made me turn around. My client had overheard my conversation and was staring at me. I thought she looked cross because she had been kept waiting. I told Nikki I would ring her later. I sat back down and apologised but the woman kept staring. Then she spoke "It's no problem. I don't know how to tell you this but I know who you are talking about. It's your Mother. My family sold the house to her."

My mouth fell open in shock. The woman took out a notepad and wrote down the address. "You will find your Mother here" she told me.

I don't remember much about the reading – only the fact that I had got my answer. After I had finished, the woman told me some more. Apparently my Mother had been confused and seemed agitated; she had made the removal men take a different route to the new house because she thought people were going to track her down and attack her. She had always been like this and it wasn't about her mental health; it was her spiritual health which was under attack.

She had felt like this since her so-called 'friend' in Jamaica had borrowed Mum's new dress. Obea had been put on the dress so when her friend returned it to my Mother, she ended up not being able to look at her own reflection. She was so distressed she started to pull out her hair. Her parents tried to help her but it is said to be rid of a bad spirit you should cross the water, which was why Mum had come to England. But now, it seemed, she was still affected by her demons.

CHAPTER 39

THE DIVINE TRUTH

Dad had been taken into hospital again; he had lost his balance and had found himself on the floor. His blood count was very low and he needed a blood transfusion to get some more haemoglobin pumped into him. His sickle cell anaemia was full blown. He was also diabetic which had adversely affected his eyes making it painful to open them.

As usual, Dad didn't complain about the pain but was, instead, short-tempered. He shouted at the nurses, telling them about themselves with various expletives, if they were heavy handed (and some were); they soon got the message.

So here I was, on a scorching hot day, looking at my Father sitting with his head in his hands. I went to look out of the window. I hadn't said a word to him. I closed my eyes and began to cry; I felt so sorry for him. Sorry for the fact that we didn't have years ahead to get to know each other. There isn't a book as yet entitled "How To Get To Know Everything About Your Father Before He Dies In Twelve Easy Steps".

Dad broke the silence. "It's strange about you and me isn't it?"

I nodded, stifling a sob.

He continued "You may try and run from me and it's no use because we both meet each other on the same path. We are linked and always will be, so why fight it? Let's not fight it any more".

I sat next to him, touched his chin and put a glass of water to his mouth; he took a few sips. This was our thing as he refused to drink or eat with the nurses. I would come in, touch his chin and he would allow me to feed him. The nurses would try the same thing but he was having none of it. Only I could do it.

I guess children have to cling on to so many threads, as few and far between that they are, to try and piece together remnants to make a patchwork quilt. This was one of the threads that attached Dad and I, and I held onto it, mentally wrapping hope around my fingers. I put the glass down and stared at him. He still had his eyes closed.

"Don't cry child. It's okay".

"I love you Dad".

"And I love you too".

That was the first, and the last, time my Father ever told me that he did.

CHAPTER 40

NO TENTS FOR TEENAGERS

Joshua was well into his teenage years (15) and I had to try very hard to meet him in the middle without beating the daylights out of him when he was being rude which would have been archaic. There are other ways to raise a child without resorting to violence.

One of my stipulations was that Josh always told me the truth – no matter what – and so far it had been put to good use on both our sides.

He had (and still has) a nice group of friends and whenever they came round to stay they were always well mannered. Teens make me laugh – when they visit other people's homes they are angelic; they leave their teenage angst for their own parents.

One of their pastimes was to pitch a tent in a field – in a 'secret location'. I didn't approve but at least he told me. However, something didn't sit right with me and I told him that sooner or later he could meet with trouble, But, teenagers sometimes need a short sharp shock to bring them round to your way of thinking.

Bob, my guide, had warned me that the field had a bad energy, and my maternal intuition thought the same.

The summer months were upon us and Josh was out and about a lot. One afternoon, I looked in on him as he sat in his bedroom. His uniform was hung up after he had come straight home from school.

He was reading Shakespeare, after which he was going to do his homework. The room smelled of lavender and primroses. Joshua smiled from ear to ear when he saw my face. He offered to wash up the plates and cups that were in his room.

Then I snapped out of my fantasy of a fantastic 'Stepford' teenager and landed back to reality with a thud. Having popped my head round his door I was acknowledged with a grunt. His entire wardrobe was on the floor. His homework was strewn across his bed and the room smelled faintly of extra mature cheese and hormones. He was playing a computer game which involved shouting "DIE! DIE! DIE!" at the screen.

"Josh, are you going out tonight?"

"Nope". But I recognised that defensive tone of voice and the body language. I was exactly the same at his age when I was lying to my back teeth.

"OK", I continued. "I'm going out for a while but I won't be long".

"How long will you be out for?" Josh asked, trying to sound laid back which rang alarm bells.

"About an hour. You can take Chef for a WALK!" I spoke loud enough that Chef jumped out of his bed, grabbed his lead and shook it around, full of anticipation.

"Aw thanks Mum. I will have to take him out now or he won't leave me alone."

Mission accomplished.

Before I left I said to him "I need to talk to you when I get back so when you finish your walk, stay put".

Stay put my arse! That child was on red alert. When a teen is planning something they put the SAS to shame. Navy Seals would shake their heads with admiration when teens are planning covert operations to overthrow the Mother Ship. I knew he would be on to his social network, be it by mobile phone or computer – or both. Some kids style it out and act all sweetness and light in front of their parents only to turn into Satan's assistants as soon as they are on the street.

When I got home Chef was barking like a maniac in the hall which he does when left on his own. I ushered him into his bed in Josh's room – as Josh had obviously gone out he should have done that before he left, so I was pretty annoyed.

In that split second I knew he had gone to that fucking field for another tent night. (On a later occasion, Josh confessed I had been standing next to the tent when I was talking to him in his room that day).

I tried to ring Josh's mobile but, of course, it was switched off. I tried some of his friends but it was the same with them. So I had to just sit this out and hope they were all okay.

The next morning I drove down a road local to where we live and saw Josh walking up, looking decidedly bedraggled with a rucksack on his back. He looked as if he hadn't slept. I pulled over.

"GET IN THE CAR!" I yelled.

He jumped out of his skin but he got in. He went to say something but I hadn't finished. "I don't want to hear anything until we get home." I am pretty sure Josh would have rather walked barefoot and blindfolded up the M1 than face me at that moment.

We got home and I stared at him. "What happened to our rule about not lying?"

He shrugged and stared at the floor. "Something happened, Mum. Shall I tell you?"

"Of course".

"Okay." He took a deep breath. "There were five of us in the tent. I needed to take a slash so I got out and stood by the hedge when I saw an outline of a man just staring at me. It was pitch dark and I didn't have my glasses but he had like a chalk outline of light around him. He made me feel scared and I walked backwards to the tent, crawled back in and whispered to the others what I had seen. They thought I was messing about until there was a thud outside and someone was hitting us through the tent. It felt like a heavy chain."

"Did he come in?" I asked.

"No Mum, he didn't. But he whispered he wanted us gone by morning then he went away; we waited for a while then we made a run for it. We left our stuff behind and went back to one of our mate's house. Sorry Mum, you were right. I won't be doing that again".

"Somebody was watching over you".

Josh nodded. "Yeah, you're right". He slowly walked to his bedroom and closed his door.

"Josh".

"Yeah?"

"You're grounded for a month".

He was about to give birth to a cow, then thought better of it. "I'll take it Mum".

"You've got no choice. NOW TIDY YOUR ROOM!"

CHAPTER 41

HUMAN NATURE

Nature is beautiful. Fortunately where I live there is plenty of woodland to walk Chef who, being a Border Collie cross, needs to be walked for a good few miles a day before he settles down at home.

All living things radiate light; that includes plants and soil. All biological substances are electrical, so it makes sense that in the past (before bricks and mortar) people lived very close to nature, absorbing all its good energy.

Everything is in perfect order in nature and if we follow its natural law we would have more affinity with ourselves and with others.

I feel that wherever anyone goes, whether dead or alive, they leave behind them an echo – a vibration of themselves. Whenever anyone visits your home they will leave an energy, which takes a while to leave.

Do you get me? No? Okay, how about when someone you love hugs you? They have their own energy, vibe, scent and if they were to go away maybe you would miss them so much as to wear their jumpers or sleep on their side of the bed. You can smell them. So let's take it further.

When someone loses a loved one through death, they may still feel them around – either through a presence or a familiar smell – tobacco or aftershave for example. This is how I feel when I walk in the woods. I always feel as if I'm being followed. Nature's spirits shimmer in and out of the trees.

A friend of mine, Terri, wanted to go to America and needed someone to look after her eight year old Jack Russell, Poppy, who was a handful to say the least. She didn't really want to leave her in kennels, but she was aware that not everyone would be able to cope with a dog that took to nipping people's ankles. So I offered to have Poppy for a week.

Poor Chef. If I had thought he would not take kindly to Poppy being in his house, he was soon put in his place by her. If he tried to go into a room she was in, she would snarl at him, bearing her tiny fangs, until he backed off. Even though Chef was about ten times her size he was petrified of her, and did as he was told.

Although they kept their place at home, it was a different story when they went for walks. They loved each other dearly. They would playfight with Chef jumping over Poppy and trying to trip her up and Poppy leaping high into the air.

If I had a busy day ahead I would walk them very early. One particular morning I took them out at about six a.m. It was still dark outside and as we got to the mouth of the woods, both dogs stopped in their tracks and refused to walk any further.

I looked up into the trees and froze. There was a tiny red light bobbing around – the best way to describe it was like a lit cigarette.

As soon as the light was aware that it was being watched, it stopped in mid air. Chef began to growl. I was frozen to the spot and as much as I wanted to move the dogs would not let me.

I thought to myself I could turn around and walk away, never returning to these woods or I could stay and watch would happen next. I knew the light was not coming from anything human, and it was still not moving. We were having a standoff.

Suddenly the light turned into a red streak and shimmered off into the woods and disappeared. Wow! It reminded me of when I was a child and saw colours in my room. I know it sounds out of this world but that is because it was.

As soon as the light disappeared the dogs relaxed. They began to walk into the woods and I had a choice. I could either run away or face my fear. I chose to face my fear and flanked by Chef and Poppy we walked further in. I was frightened but I had to do it otherwise I would not walk in there again at that time of the morning.

There is something sacred about dawn. The colours of the night and day are merged, and it's like a meditation, when I put the world to rights in my head, to problem solve and wonder what that day will bring.

CHAPTER 42

PADRE

Since our talk in the hospital, Dad's and my relationship was a lot better. I told him that I had seen Mum and he said "Why?"

"Why not?"

"That woman gave me a hard time".

"According to Mum you weren't exactly the love of her life either." I retorted.

He laughed and shrugged his shoulders. "I don't care."

But I knew he was covering his true feelings and, when he looked at me, he understood.

I tried to lighten the mood. "Seen any ghosts lately Dad?"

He laughed and shook his head.

CHAPTER 43

MADRE

In-between visiting Dad I was seeing Mum. It was weird but throughout my life more often than not I would always end up seeing them both at the same time, no matter how long the time had been.

I knocked on my Mother's door and she opened it almost immediately. I walked in and sat on the sofa. It was kind of my safety net – to sit down quickly and try to assemble my thoughts and keep my feelings in check. My Mother was eying me up and down looking for something that I couldn't see. She asked "Where's your son?"

"Joshua's at school".

"Oh. So where are you living now?"

"Surrey".

"Surrey is a big place. Where?"

I looked at the floor; I didn't want to say where I lived just in case she hunted me down and snatched me away. Bob was right. I had to have a showdown with my Mother. Besides, what was I doing there anyway? What was I looking for? For Mum to turn into a model mother and love me? It was too late for that. At some point I would need the showdown but not today.

However, as I looked at her, I felt the first stirrings of change within me. Anger was building up in the pit of my stomach. And within half an hour I was making for the door with Mum standing watching me. I was nearly ready. But what worried me was how far would it go?

CHAPTER 44

BETTY

Mary is a good friend of mine. We have been friends for a long time but for some reason she didn't know what I did – the contact with the dead. When we met up we talked about everything else but that.

Mary was originally from Nunhead, close to Peckham (South London) where I used to live. We were cut from the same cloth, and had got on famously from the first time we met in Cinderella Rockerfellas, a nightclub in Purley, Surrey.

Mary ran the nightclub restaurant and some were a little wary of her as she spoke her mind. But I saw past that and we would have a great laugh. If my feet ached due to my high stilettos, Mary had a spare pair that I could wear towards the middle of the evening. They were silver with a small heel and my toes would stretch with relief, having been jammed in pointed shoes for hours.

Mary wanted me to meet her Mum, Betty, so I was taken to Nunhead where she still lived. She was a very friendly tiny woman with a love for her daughter which was great to see. We stayed for a while and chatted. Betty made me feel so welcome it was as if we had met before.

When it was time to leave Betty stood at the door and waved Mary and me 'goodbye'. That was the first and last time I saw her as Betty died a few years later.

So now Mary, Joshua and I were having lunch in a shopping precinct. Joshua was quite young then and was sitting in his pushchair. We were idly chatting when it happened. Mary's Mum's energy was building up around her. It's hard to explain but I'll try. It's like looking at shimmering heat on a hot summer's day. It's like a vortex – waves of energy, like a wind.

How did I know it was Betty? I just knew. It's a knowing. And her sprit told me. Her love for her daughter resonated through her presence. She was taking no prisoners. Mary was chatting away and I all I could hear over her voice was Betty gently urging me to tell Mary she was with us.

We finally got in the car to go home and Betty continued to tell me to say to Mary she was with us. I shot Mary a sideward's glance. I closed my eyes and took a deep breath.

"Mary, you know how I used to mess about at Cinderella's and tell people their fortunes? I really was doing it but I hadn't realised to what depth or how far it would go. I wouldn't hurt you in any way right? But I have to tell you that your Mum is here and she wants you to know she's okay". Mary stopped talking – which was unusual! I went on. "Your Mum's telling me that she has your dogs with her. The ones that slept on a tartan blanket".

For as long as I can remember Mary has owned a dog – she adores them. She nodded, not saying anything.

"You are making a dark blue velvet curtain to hang against the front door of your old flat for the new tenant".

Mary's eyes filled with tears. "Go on".

"Your Mum is standing next to a woman that is not very happy that your Mum is talking to me. She was religious and is standing in front of a green wall; she used to look after parrots. But your Mum is insisting that she talks to me."

Then she disappeared from my head. Mary confirmed that the woman with her Mum was her aunt, Betty's sister. She was a staunch Catholic and indeed had kept parrots. Her old house had a room with green walls. She lived on her own and died a spinster.

Mary's eyes then filled with tears of happiness.

A few months later Mary came to my home. She talked about that day in the car and said "Thank you so much. You've helped me come to terms with the loss of my Mother. I want you to have one of her rings". She handed me a beautiful sapphire ring surrounded by diamonds.

We both began to cry and I could feel Betty around us. She whispered "Thank you".

CHAPTER 45

DANNY – GENIUS OF LOVE

What can I say about Danny? Quite a lot actually. I could write a whole book about him. I was privileged to meet him after he had passed over only a few weeks previously, just shy of his twenty-second birthday and, as you can imagine, his poor Mum, Mandy, was distraught. She wanted to know that he was all right. It was a miracle that Danny had lived as long as he did, because he was born with multiple disabilities.

All Mandy heard when Danny was born were the nurses saying he would be better off dead because of his health problems. He had microcephaly (small head), multiple congenital abnormalities, bilateral cleft lip and palate, Pierre Robin Sequence, pigeon chest on one side and slightly protruding chest on the other, osteoporosis and chronic lung disease for which he required a tracheostomy. I only list these conditions because, although it's none of our business, he wanted to live even with the difficulties he would face. As soon as Mandy looked into his eyes for the first time, he reached into her soul and she was smitten.

The nurses' voices faded away. Danny looked frail but his strength was immense and his soul beautiful. Although he couldn't talk or hardly move, people who knew him could see his qualities shining through; and, as his mother said, he made her stronger, and more empathetic to people who appear broken to the outside world.

Mandy had other children and her husband to also look after but there was no way Danny would go into an institution. She did not have a break until she found someone she could trust 100% to look after and love him as much as his family did.

One day, that special person came into their lives – Danielle, who I am sure Danny chose. They met at school and bonded instantly. Danny really enjoyed her company and Danielle could see what others couldn't which was his amazing personality. Mandy was so happy that they had her in their lives.

As any Medium will tell you, when it comes to readings for children from any age (0 upwards) it is so emotive you really have to be on your A Game, keeping feelings in check. When Danny contacted Mandy, the love for his Mum filled the room we were in, which happened to be his bedroom. I looked up and saw a beautiful silk parachute on the ceiling. It was light and airy and I could feel Danny's presence everywhere. When I first saw him, he was in a wheelchair but then he stood up, pushed it away and hugged his Mum. This is when the reading for me became ground breaking. He passed on a few messages that his Mum could relate to. I then asked him through thought "How did you feel living on Earth in a body you were trapped in?"

"I was never trapped. I was able to travel around in my astral body. I could go wherever I wanted. Would you like me to show you?"

I nodded. I began to feel as if my brain was plugged into a socket and an amplifier switched on. I felt trapped in my body for a few seconds but then flew out. I was seeing "A day in the life of Danny", floating around his home, zooming outside and bobbing around in fields speeding up as if I was flying in a helicopter. It was amazing.

Then Danny pulled the plug out of my mind and I felt like myself again. What a wonderful lad.

During another reading with both Mandy and Danielle, Danny came up with the idea that they work together for charity. We thought this was a great idea as Mandy still had so much to give. When she played back the recording of the reading Danny whispered "Pay attention, pay attention". He really wanted his idea to be taken seriously.

He also said Danielle had lost an earring. I relayed this and she replied "Yes, I lost one of the Angel earrings that Mandy got me so she bought me another pair but I lost one of those as well; but now at least I've still got a pair".

Mandy said "Danny's got them" and on the recording Danny can be heard saying "I've got them, I've got them".

Now you will be thinking if Danny couldn't speak on Earth how did we know it was him? It's because of his vibration. He was sent to teach us to love more and open our hearts. I have so much respect for this young soul that there are not enough words to truly go him justice.

CHAPTER 46

AN AUDIENCE WITH ...

Mitcham Spiritualist Church in South London is a warm and friendly place. Some of my clients attended the Spiritualist Circle that was held there once a week on a Wednesday. I was invited to the Circle and I thoroughly enjoyed it. The people were friendly and the proof of messages was outstanding.

The person who ran the Circle asked if I would like to do a stint of some platform work. That means standing on stage and giving messages to an audience. My ego was way ahead of the game and I found myself saying "yes". With hindsight, which is wonderful, I would never have agreed. But of course I had been caught up in the moment of the great Circle and I was on a roll.

And so it was arranged I would be a medium for the evening. On my own. I could not believe I had let this happen. Give me a microphone and I will sing into it – no problem. But giving messages to an audience – oh my goodness, no way!

I was in way over my head. I asked whether I could get out of it. But it had already been booked. Maybe I could walk on the stage and pretend to fall off? No, it would end up bad. I would pay for it with pain. The day was looming and I was in a right tizzy. What should I wear? How would I come across to the congregation? Would I fart? And worst of all, would any spirit or spirits talk to me? I turned to Bob to see what he had to say on the matter but he was silent. That meant he had something up his sleeve.

At last the evening arrived. The congregation was pretty large. I took my friend to one side and asked "Are they all here for me?"

"Yes, it's great isn't it?"

I thought to myself "Great. I'll need a medium in a minute for when I drop dead with fright to apologise on my behalf".

Then in no time I heard "And tonight's medium is Jassmine James".

I wanted to throw up over the compere's head but found myself standing next to him. I honestly cannot remember much about it, only snatches. I saw Bob standing to my left. I said to him in thought "At fucking last! I've been trying to hold of you for yonks and you come to me now? When I wanted to talk to you before? Thanks a lot."

He smiled. "Keep calm child, I have spirits here who need to contact the group of people in front of you. Trust and stop chasing your heart. Just talk, it will be all right". He started to laugh. So he was laughing at me now? Thanks Bob.

I opened my mouth to try and form a sound and heard myself saying "I would like to come to this lady here". She was quite old and I could see an old man in spirit standing next to her. Bob told me his name was Henry and he had had his funeral recently. I told the lady "There is a man standing next to you called Henry. He says he has only been in spirit for a short time".

Her jaw dropped and she shouted in a thick guttural German accent "'enry? 'enry? I only buried 'im yesterday afternoon! Do deh come through so soon?"

"So it seems" I replied.

I cannot remember much after that. I just have a faint memory of spirit folk making their way towards me and Bob keeping them in an orderly queue whilst they waited for me to connect them with their loved ones.

CHAPTER 47

SET IT OFF

Walking into my Mother's house was always like going to the mouth of a lion. She let me in and I sat down on the edge of the sofa. The jacket I was wearing was heaving with the extra weight I was carrying. This was a side effect of seeing both my parents at the same time. I was eating to insulate the feelings that I couldn't process. Being a blimp was the perfect buffer.

Before visiting my Mother I would eat something savoury and salty. My stomach was gurgling in protest at the crap it was being fed.

Mum said "You look good. It's nice to see you so fat".

I thought "Why would you say that to your own child?"

She went off to get a drink and at that moment everything fell into place. While I was fat I wasn't a threat. When I was super slim my Mum wasn't just envious – she was so jealous that when I was small she would tell me I was bony and should eat more. My sister, Diane, told me later that Mum wanted the superb physique she had had in her youth.

Mum stood in the doorway and asked the usual "Have you seen Louis? And have you got money?"

I smiled. "I've got enough".

Both my parents had the same opinions on a problem – throw money at it and it will go away.

Mum went upstairs and I wandered around the room. All the blood, sweat and tears that my Mother had worked for all her life, just to be in this mess – which was all of her own making. She wasn't at peace with herself, the pleasure of earning all that money and acquiring houses. What good did it do? She knew she would never be at peace while she lived on Earth.

She came back down and I stared her in the eyes. I could only feel anger which rose from the roots of my soul. It rumbled like a herd of stampeding buffalo and threatened to trample both me and my Mother. The room shifted slightly and the energy changed. I closed my eyes and saw Bob standing between us. He was wearing black warpaint was across his face and white smoke surrounded him. This was the time – the moment. I was ready to confront my Mother about my past.

My voice took on an unusual tone. It was deeper. I became the High Priestess. I looked into her eyes and she stared me down, but then Bob caught her eye. She glanced at him and then looked at me.

"You're still not doing that shit are you?"

I sat up, my shoulders square, my jaw strong. "I am". My gaze did not waiver. I continued "Mother, do you regret what you did to me, and what you did to Diane and Louis?"

There was an eerie silence. Something snapped and I wanted to kill her. I wanted to wring the life out of her. [My sister Diane had felt the same when Mum had trapped her in the hallway, threatening to smash her face in. Diane was ready to kill her but stopped herself as she didn't want to be jailed].

The same happened to me. Rationality came to the rescue. I had no fear of her. Whatever Karmic chains had linked us in the past through many lifetimes I felt them break. The debt had been paid in full. I breathed and closed my eyes, waiting for her response.

"No. I don't regret a thing that I have done to you. Do you know why? Because you deserved it".

I sprang up like a she-wolf and stood face to face with her. I knew she wanted to strike me but I wasn't a little girl any more – I was a woman. My lips curled back into a snarl. I nudged her with my shoulder. She stepped back. All my life I had been so polite to her out of deference – just for the fact she was my Mother. I pushed her again. She had lost.

"Goodbye *Mother*".

I walked out of the house knowing I would only see her again in death. I cried for all the times she had beaten me, my brother and my sister. I cried for all the times I felt so insecure and like I was a piece of shit. Louis, Diane and I were all broken and we were all trying desperately to heal.

She was no longer 'Mother' but Cynthia. Her only maternal role was to give birth to me.

Bob came to me. "This is your time. This is now the time to heal. You have won. Well done. You can kill a person a thousand times without striking them once. Now be who are you are supposed to be, not who you think you were. Trust in what you do because you have a gift like no other. It's unique to you that you have been through so many trials and tribulations. Every test that has been put before you, you have won. This is your prize – the present you give yourself. You have been given life. Now start again". Bob faded away.

I was born that day and it was painful, but I was willing to relearn – to walk, to talk, to think. This was my time.

CHAPTER 48

NAKED TO THE WORLD

Now that Cynthia was dealt with I felt like a newborn child, placed at the feet of fresh chapter and verse. I was scared to death. But in the core of my heart I knew that God and all his Angels were there. Yeah I got my swagger but I walked a little slower. I was learning, living, breathing for the first time. I was at my Father's house and sat staring at him as he slept. He stirred a little, opened his eyes and looked into mine.

"What's troubling you?" he asked.

I shook my head and cried.

He gently touched my arm. "Don't cry. It will be all right".

"I know it will".

It was my spiritual birthday. Born before the mouth of the Universe. Naked to the world.

CHAPTER 49

ILL WINDS, ARE BLOWING ME NO GOOD

My Mother passed over in 2007, eight years after that last meeting. I knew she had passed because she came to tell me, as I related in the first chapter. Although I hadn't been told officially at this point (I was to hear exactly one year later) I felt like my Mother was more dangerous than ever, because wherever she may be was not a good place. She kept telling me this in my sleep. Nightmares of her banging my bedroom walls, with a wind cold as ice howling through my body. She was trying to reach out for help and forgiveness but I couldn't give it.

We battled for months with her whispering then shouting my name. It was so frightening. I begged for her to be taken away but she wouldn't leave. I would wake to see a dark shadow in the corner, and Chef would not go anywhere near my bedroom. I begged Bob for help but he told me "This is your battle. Fight her. She cannot hurt you; she has to find forgiveness in herself and in you so she can move on. You must break the chains that bind you, so that you can both be free".

It continued for another month. I stood up to her and begged "Find your path to the light. Please give me peace. There will be a time when I can forgive you".

CHAPTER 50

MOTHER MAY I

In 2008, I officially got word of my Mother's death, after my brother Louis tracked me down via the Salvation Army who had asked me to contact them.

The man I called asked me a few questions including my date of birth to ascertain he was speaking to the right person. He took a breath and said "I have something to tell you".

"My Mother has passed away".

He spluttered, "How did you know?"

"I just know".

He paused, and then said warily "Very well. We will make contact with Louis".

I met up with Louis that afternoon. Incredibly we were living just ten minutes apart. We picked up where we left off, as per usual.

"How did she die Lou?" I asked.

"On her own. They found her half hanging off the bed. She had been there for approximately two weeks. Maggots crawling out of her".

I got no joy from hearing that. Poor Mum dying alone and frightened.

Her funeral had been a simple affair. People who she had known from her days in Jamaica who had also moved to England paid their respects. When I was ten years old I told my Mother I would never go to her funeral and, even if I had had the choice, I would not have gone.

My sister Diane went into auto pilot and got the job done. She was constantly reminded how much she looked like Mum. It made my sister sick to her stomach. At funerals people will pretty much always evangelise the dead person.

Louis didn't say much about Mums' funeral but one of my cousins Em said she had been suffering and in pain. Em had asked her what was wrong and was told it was "Atonement and retribution for what I did to my children". She was feeling the turmoil in her soul. Poor Mum. She had suffered a massive stroke.

CHAPTER 51

DOING THINGS TOGETHER
THE MOTHER AND FATHER EXPERIENCE

My parents had always done things in synch within at least eighteen months to two years of each other. Therefore, I knew my Father would pass in a matter of months.

I was having a totally different experience with him than I had had with my Mother. He was never physically violent to me but he was verbally aggressive, so I had to be on my guard. But things were becoming much easier. We had found a common ground. We were getting there even though there was not enough time to heal everything between us. I told Dad about Mum's death. He didn't miss a beat. He kissed his teeth and said "Boy, that woman she did give me a hard time." He pursed his lips, crossed his arms and shot a sideward glace at me. I knew deep down he still loved her. "Clever woman though".

I shook my head. "Dad"

"What?"

"Nothing".

CHAPTER 52

HOMEWARD BOUND

Dad took another fall and this time he totally lost his bearings and had smashed a side table lamp, nearly causing a fire. When more accidents followed. I had made the decision to put him into a home which I hated doing, but I just could not have him live with me. I felt so guilty.

Dad had another daughter, Javeena, who is older than me. She lived in Jamaica for the first fourteen years of her life until her mother sent for her to live in America, where she settled.

Dad was becoming slightly demented. This cruel illness would give him rare lucid moments but on the whole he could not look after himself. Javeena came over from Florida to help make the final decision. Sad as it was, he had to go into a care home.

Dad had to be assessed by a social worker and, on this particular day, he was not only lucid but on top form. However, I knew better; he would be confused tomorrow. The social worker said he was not to be put into a home and everyone looked at me accusingly.

Unfortunately over the next few months Dad fell so many times I lost count. Then he nearly blew himself up when he tried to light the cooker to make a cup of tea. I kept silent and continued trying to help. No, I am not Little Eva in the snow playing poor me, I just didn't want my Father to die alone through an accident when it was avoidable.

Eventually, I got a call from social services who were concerned about Dad. They felt he should be put in a home. I said rather sarcastically "You think?"

CHAPTER 53

THE DIVINE TRUTH PART II

Dad went into a home providing twenty-four hours of "care". I use the term loosely as it was never fantastic. There were a few carers who knew what that word actually meant, and one was Olu whom my Father warmed to. Olu had his own cross to bear. His face was twisted on one side and he walked with a limp. However he was the most handsome man I had met. His beauty shone through every pore.

On this particular day, Dad was in difficulty due to his blood count being low. I phoned his local hospital and wanted to know why they were not giving Dad a blood transfusion. even though his health was deteriorating fast; he was having palliative care and should have been made as comfortable as possible. He was dying so they didn't think it was 'worth it'. How dare they - they would have treated a dog better.

Olu was tending to Dad as I walked in to his private room. He greeted me with a smile and I asked how Dad had been.

Olu replied Dad was very confused due to lack of haemoglobin. Having full blown sickle cell he should have been entitled to a transfusion so Olu helped me get through the red tape and I spoke to the top blood consultant. After I asserted my authority (shouted) Dad was to be admitted the next day.

When I made the call I looked and felt like shit. Tears filled my eyes. Olu was looking at me and cleared his throat. He said "I want to tell you something. I know you are struggling with your Father. He is difficult at times and he was not always there for you. But he has chosen you and only you to see him through to the next world. Your ancestors have called upon you to do this. You see, I know and understand. I was born like this. The seventh child. My embarrassed parents sent me to the UK to be looked after by my auntie. Then 10 years later the rest of the family came over. My brothers bullied me for years but I couldn't defend myself because of my twisted body. As soon as I was able I made my own life and now I have a beautiful wife and identical twin boys; we are a happy family. My brothers do not have it so good. Between them they disrespect our parents, have not been able to earn money or keep relationships. My parents come to me with their hands open so I look after them. But they are not allowed in my home or welcome or involved in anything in my life. You are the one that God has chosen to be with your Father. If you do this you will be blessed one thousand times."

"Thanks Olu". I dried my tears, went to Dad's room, tapped his chin and gave him a drink of water.

CHAPTER 54

LET'S DANCE THE LAST DANCE WITH MY FATHER

Dad was worn out. He had had all the blood transfusions he would ever need and wanted to make the last transition.

My sister was not in the country but she needed to come over if she wanted to say her goodbye to our Father.

Dad was in hospital and this was it. I knew by next week he would be gone. I gently tapped his chin and he sipped the water I offered. He was in and out of consciousness. Javeena came over with her husband and son.

No one had warned them how Dad would look and when I walked into his room I got a cool reception.

Javeena said "Have you seen Dad's bed sores?"

In all honesty, with everything that had been going on, I hadn't.

At least now Javeena was here to take turns to stay with Dad and make sure he was comfortable.

A few days later Javeena telephoned me "You need to come now". I knew Dad was leaving us. I jumped in the car and drove like a maniac, jumping two red traffic lights. Then I saw my Father sitting next to me, still wearing his hospital gown. He said "Slow down. I'm gone".

I screamed "No. You were supposed to wait. I was supposed to be there".

I drove even faster. The angels of travel guided me and I got to the hospital in one piece. I rushed to the ward. Javeena was in the waiting room and she called after me "Don't go in. He's gone".

I sobbed. Dad. My Dad. I ran to his ward screaming all the way down the corridor. I came to him and fell on his body. I whispered "No one can hurt you now. Go in peace my Dad". I leant my ear against his chest. His heart was still. I prayed to God to make it start again but I knew he was all right.

I held his hand and looked at his thumbs. I whispered "See Dad, we still have the same thumbs". I gently measured my fingers against his. A nurse was trying to give me water. Javeena was staring. She couldn't touch him and you know what? That was okay. She had things to deal with.

Everything was peaceful. We went back to Dad's home and I sat in his chair and soaked up his presence.

CHAPTER 55

CAR DANCING WITH MY FATHER

I felt really numb. I wanted the world to stop. I turned on the radio thinking of Dad. He wasn't a father, he couldn't do it but somehow we had made peace with each other. I think it was because I stopped looking for him to be a dad, and saw him as a human being who had fucked up along the way.

The one thing that we both loved was dancing. Luther Vandross' 'Dance With My Father' will always remind me of him and as I waited in the traffic there it was. Luther singing his sweet melody

> *"I'd play a song that would never ever end,*
> *How I'd love love love.*
> *To dance with my father again"*

I sobbed "Dad, well done. I know you're all right". I could feel him in the car and it was good.

Then a few days later I was emptying the washing machine, zoning out and behind me I could feel Dad's presence. He pushed the door open and said "I'm ok". I couldn't turn around. He said "Bye love".

"Bye Dad".

CHAPTER 56

THE FORGIVEN

My parents, God love them, had died within 2 years of each other. The tag team had finally caught up with one another and now it was April 14th 2011 to be exact. Dad had been dead for a few months and Mum seemed to have quietened down. I was busy writing *Sunflowers*, propped up in bed. I felt a creative burst that morning and I was on a roll. Words tumbling over each other begging to be written. I was thinking about how James Cameron had written Avatar in a matter of weeks. I could understand that. The creative door was kicked open and I was taking full advantage of it.

Then I felt a swirl of energy in the corner of the room. I thought "No, not a spirit. Please. I need to write". It was forming and then I saw her. It was my Mother. She materialised and she looked beautiful. She had been through the fire and made peace with her soul. I couldn't breathe. She stepped forward, touched my face and caught a tear running down my cheek.

"Please forgive me," she said.

I stared into her eyes. She was pure, cleansed. God had welcomed her back into His arms

"You – are – forgiven".

She smiled and faded away from me. I felt so light in my heart I could have flown up to the sky. I was free and could breathe. My childhood spirit was allowed to dance again in the sun. Whatever I am I still have my parents within me. I chose to forgive because forgiveness heals.

Much love to all.

Namaste om shanti shanti shanti.

Peace Peace Peace.

Love Jassmine.

Lightning Source UK Ltd.
Milton Keynes UK
UKHW020632140420
361671UK00005B/350

9 781326 347918